TEACHING for LIFELONG LEARNING

How to Prepare Students
for a Changing World

ELLIOTT SEIF

foreword by Jay McTighe

Solution Tree | Press

a division of
Solution Tree

Copyright © 2021 by Elliott Seif

Materials appearing here are copyrighted. With one exception, all rights are reserved. Readers may reproduce only those pages marked "Reproducible." Otherwise, no part of this book may be reproduced or transmitted in any form or by any means (electronic, photocopying, recording, or otherwise) without prior written permission of the publisher.

555 North Morton Street
Bloomington, IN 47404
800.733.6786 (toll free) / 812.336.7700
FAX: 812.336.7790

email: info@SolutionTree.com

SolutionTree.com

Visit **go.SolutionTree.com/21stcenturyskills** to download the free reproducibles in this book.

Printed in the United States of America

Library of Congress Cataloging-in-Publication Data

Names: Seif, Elliott, author.
Title: Teaching for lifelong learning : how to prepare students for a
   changing world / Elliott Seif.
Description: Bloomington, IN : Solution Tree Press, [2021] | Includes
   bibliographical references and index.
Identifiers: LCCN 2020046088 | ISBN 9781951075477 (paperback) | ISBN
   9781951075484 (ebook)
Subjects: LCSH: Critical thinking--Study and teaching. | Problem
   solving--Study and teaching. | Student-centered learning. | Curriculum
   enrichment. | Learning, Psychology of.
Classification: LCC LB1590.3 .S36 2021 | DDC 371.39/4--dc23
LC record available at https://lccn.loc.gov/2020046088

Solution Tree
Jeffrey C. Jones, CEO
Edmund M. Ackerman, President

Solution Tree Press
President and Publisher: Douglas M. Rife
Associate Publisher: Sarah Payne-Mills
Art Director: Rian Anderson
Managing Production Editor: Kendra Slayton
Copy Chief: Jessi Finn
Senior Production Editor: Tonya Maddox Cupp
Content Development Specialist: Amy Rubenstein
Copy Editor: Mark Hain
Proofreader: Elisabeth Abrams
Text and Cover Designer: Kelsey Hergül
Editorial Assistants: Sarah Ludwig and Elijah Oates

Acknowledgments

This book is a labor of love, built on my many years of numerous positive encounters with wonderful educational leaders and teachers all across the country and abroad.

My deepest thanks go to all who helped contribute to this book. To single out a few: my many wise professors, especially Don Oliver, Fred Newmann, Harold Berlak, Louis Smith, and Arthur Wirth; my many thoughtful graduate school colleagues; the many professors who taught with me at Temple University, especially Bob McCollum, the inquiry guru, who died too early in a plane crash over Lockerbie, Scotland in 1988; and so many wonderful educators, too numerous to mention individually, who led and taught in the Bucks County schools. Special thanks to my colleagues at the Bucks County Intermediate Unit, among them Jim LoGiudice, Larry Martin, Jeanette Warsavage, and Karen Steinbrink. I thank the many dedicated, wonderful leaders and teachers in the School District of Philadelphia, especially those at the Science Leadership Academy and the Parkway Northwest High School for Peace and Social Justice. Jay McTighe, Grant Wiggins (who is unfortunately no longer with us), and all the dedicated members of the Understanding by Design cadre that I worked with over many years have been wonderful, thoughtful, and caring colleagues and friends.

I am also indebted to so many authors of books and articles, many of them referenced in this book, that have advanced the educational profession, and to the many schools and districts that I visited and with which I worked. There were so many wonderful and dedicated leaders and teachers who opened up their classrooms and schools, shared their knowledge and experiences, and showed me what it means to have an excellent school and be an excellent teacher.

I also dedicate this book to my family—to my wonderful wife, Ellie, who puts up with my intensity and concentration; my daughters and their families—Deborah, Karen, Christine, CJ, and Marcus—and my many friends and acquaintances who tolerate my fervent discussions about education and are willing to share their own educational experiences and ideas with me.

My deepest thanks go to Solution Tree Press for its unwavering support for this book and its ideas. In particular, my thanks go to my first editor, Amy Rubenstein, whose editing skills were so valuable in helping me refine and clarify my thoughts and ideas, and to Tonya Cupp, who so ably walked me through the final editing and production of the book.

Finally, I want to thank the many students whom I have observed and spoken with over the years who gave me so many insights into the challenges of schooling and the reasons why education must keep up with the times. This book is for them.

Solution Tree Press would like to thank the following reviewers:

Rita Fischer
Assistant Superintendent for
 Curriculum and Instruction
Community High School District 128
Vernon Hills, Illinois

Kim Tucker
Supervisor of Curriculum and
 Instruction
Somers Point School District
Somers Point, New Jersey

Jeremy Muse
Principal
Lake Elementary School
St. Amant, Louisiana

Visit **go.SolutionTree.com/21stcenturyskills** to download the free reproducibles in this book.

Table of Contents

Reproducible pages appear in italics.

CHAPTER 2

Adapting Instruction for Lifelong Learning 41

CHAPTER 3

Assessing for Lifelong Learning 81

CHAPTER 4

Developing a Lifelong Learning Curriculum 105

CHAPTER 5

Including Project–Based Learning and Civics Education

About the Author

Elliott Seif, PhD, is an educational consultant, author, school volunteer, and public school advocate. He was a social studies teacher, a professor of education at Temple University, and the Director of Curriculum and Instruction Services for the Bucks County Intermediate Unit, an educational service agency for Bucks County, Pennsylvania.

At the Bucks County Intermediate Unit, Seif provided leadership in curriculum and instruction training and reform, and he developed, led, or participated in more than fifty program reviews for Bucks County school districts. He has conducted professional development programs with numerous schools and school districts throughout the United States and abroad on a variety of topics, including standards-based education, thinking-skill development, instructional improvement, assessment issues, and curriculum development using Understanding by Design (UbD).

Seif is the author of many books, handbooks, articles, commentaries, and reports, including a textbook on the teaching of elementary social studies. His published articles include "Social Studies Revived" and "You Can Teach for Meaning" (with Jay McTighe and Grant Wiggins) in *Educational Leadership*, the journal of the Association for Supervision and Curriculum Development (ASCD). He and Jay McTighe also coauthored a chapter, "An Implementation Framework to Support

TEACHING FOR LIFELONG LEARNING

21st Century Skills," in *21st Century Skills: Rethinking How Students Learn* for Solution Tree Press.

Seif was also a member of the ASCD Understanding by Design cadre and the ASCD UbD faculty. He has assisted numerous schools and school districts throughout the United States and abroad in using UbD to improve educational practice and co-taught ASCD UbD professional development institutes with Jay McTighe, codeveloper of UbD.

Seif has received many awards for his accomplishments, including from ASCD, the Pennsylvania Association of Intermediate Units, the Pennsylvania Association for Supervision and Curriculum Development, and the Bucks County schools.

Seif received a master of education degree from Harvard University and a doctorate from Washington University in St. Louis in curriculum research and development.

To learn more about Elliott Seif's work, visit www.lifelonglearninged.org or follow @elliottseif on Twitter.

To book Elliott Seif for professional development, contact pd@SolutionTree.com.

Foreword

By Jay McTighe

I am writing this foreword near the end of the 2020 calendar year as the world remains in the grip of the coronavirus pandemic. This unexpected and catastrophic phenomenon has resulted in more than a million and a half deaths worldwide to date, caused global economic turmoil, and disrupted all facets of normal life. Sadly, the pandemic offers a sobering reminder to educators that we are no longer educating students for a stable and predictable world. To the contrary—modern schooling must equip learners to face an increasingly complex, interconnected, and unpredictable world. No longer will success be determined by who can remember the most or who scores highest on standardized tests. Indeed, this book's title signals its focus on preparing students to understand key concepts, to transfer their learning, and to keep learning new things independently.

This book is conceptually rich and centers on the need to prepare students for a lifetime of learning. Dr. Seif defines and describes why this is necessary and illustrates the process of a lifelong learning education with a description of research-based learning principles (that he and I developed together) and rich examples of learning from the world of gaming, music, and sports. These critical ideas are then brought to life through an impressively comprehensive discussion on how they impact educational goals, teaching methods, assessment practices, and curriculum development. He introduces a practical and proven four-phase instructional model featuring a variety of interactive techniques that teachers can use to engage learners in active meaning making. Additional online resources supplement the many and varied samples that are provided in the text.

Dr. Seif's long and rich career includes time as a teacher, administrator, curriculum director, college professor, and national consultant that has prepared him to author this important work. He combines the scholarship and research acumen of an academic with the practicality of a lifelong educator working in, and with, both public and private schools. Seif walks his talk. While endorsing the use of thoughtful classroom questions to engage learners in making meaning, he includes reflection questions, along with suggested action steps, at the conclusion of each chapter to actively engage his readers in making sense of the text and making plans to apply its ideas.

In sum, *Teaching for Lifelong Learning* is rich in ideas for a modern learning system. The education world is flooded with new publications on every conceivable topic—yet not all are of equal value. To invoke a cuisine-based analogy: if the plethora of educational blog posts provide snacks, and articles in educational journals offer a quick lunch, this book provides a gourmet meal—with a selection of fine wines and dessert. So, begin your reading with a hearty appetite for learning and savor each delectable chapter!

Introduction

If we teach today's students as we taught yesterday's, we rob them of tomorrow.

—John Dewey

Have you ever played a video game? Most games have levels—easiest to play at level one, hardest at the highest level. With continued and persistent practice, a player gradually improves the required skills over time, and moves to the next level. The higher the level, the more challenging and complicated the game. Mastery requires practice.

It seems to me that school should be like that, too. Students begin at initial levels of learning in the early grades by learning how to read, learning new vocabulary and concepts, developing an understanding of the natural and social world through science and social studies, and exploring the arts. Students should also have the opportunity, at an early age, to develop and practice skills as researchers, writers, listeners, collaborators, and thinkers. As they develop content knowledge, understanding, skills, and behaviors and attitudes that promote learning, they are increasingly challenged. They—hopefully—continually improve their abilities to interpret, analyze, and synthesize knowledge and develop a more sophisticated understanding of key ideas. They get opportunities to write more analytically and persuasively. Ideally, they learn to solve complex problems and be creative and original in their thinking. Also, as they develop a knowledge and skill base, they should learn both independently and interdependently. By graduation at grade 12, they should be curious explorers who are interested in learning, ask good questions, conduct solid research, think critically and creatively, and communicate well. In other words, they should be good at learning to learn—to be able to do their work and learn at high levels both independently and collaboratively.

Research on how people learn supports this more active, growth-oriented way of thinking about learning (Bransford, Brown, & Cocking, 1999; Colvin, 2008; Dweck, 2006, 2015; Hattie, 2012; Mehta & Fine, 2019; National Research Council, 2005; Shenk, 2010). In *Mindset: The New Psychology of Success*, Carol S. Dweck (2006) describes how the development of a growth mindset, instead of a fixed mindset, enables students to seek challenge and thrive on change. Citing considerable research, educators and authors Jal Mehta and Sarah Fine (2019) suggest that teachers need to help students explore, conjecture, and construct their own learning. They need to "bring to the fore student thinking . . .and create a collaborative culture in which this kind of thinking and learning can thrive" (pp. 13–14). Engagement, motivation, interest—even passion for learning—become important. Basing its assertion on the latest research, the National Academies of Sciences, Engineering, and Medicine (2018) describes learning this way:

> "Learn" is an active verb; it is something people do, not something that happens to them. People are not passive recipients of learning, even if they are not always aware that the learning process is happening. Instead, through acting in the world, people encounter situations, problems, and ideas. By engaging with these situations, problems, and ideas, they have social, emotional, cognitive, and physical experiences, and they adapt. These experiences and adaptations shape a person's abilities, skills, and inclinations going forward, thereby influencing and organizing that individual's thoughts and actions into the future. (p. 12)

This active, growth-oriented way of thinking about teaching and learning is also critical to preparing students for a changing world and an uncertain future. Since the early 1980s, the relentlessly changing economy, with growth built around new technologies and innovation, has emphasized the development of information, technology, and service-based workplaces (Moretti, 2013). Good jobs in health care, finance, technology, and even industry usually require higher-level skill sets. Manufacturing jobs often require significant science, technology, engineering, and mathematics (STEM) skills. Millions of people no longer work a full-time job: they are contract workers, adapting to continuously developing new opportunities and gaining employment through their own proactive initiative (Wakabayashi, 2019).

Many become entrepreneurs and start their own businesses, which require high levels of specialized knowledge, research, thinking, creativity, and communication skills. Continuing education that is geared to new types of training and upgrading of skills is critical.

Artificial intelligence is changing the very nature of how machines communicate with humans, both increasing the power of human thinking and substituting machine thinking for human thinking. The Human Genome Project (National Human Genome Research Institute, n.d.) has changed the way we think about life itself. Climate changes are affecting the lives of billions around the world as the earth warms, the seas rise, and the weather intensifies. The COVID-19 virus pandemic seriously disrupted the lives of billions of people around the world (World Health Organization, 2020). We are unsure of what its lasting results will be on the economy, culture, and politics.

The way students need to be prepared to participate in civic life has also changed. There has been an explosion of civic information and ideas, with very diverse points of view and a lot of suspect information and propaganda. Citizens from the U.S. and elsewhere across the world need broad knowledge about the basics of history, economics, government, and democratic values, and deeper knowledge and understanding of fundamental citizenship understandings and skills. All citizens need a working knowledge of scientific topics and the methods science uses to validate information, as well as the skills needed to understand and sort through the complexities of many challenging issues, such as health care, immigration, international relations, economic inequality, and education. Citizens must have an understanding of the market economy and the economic complexity of a modern society, both local and global. It is also critical for every citizen to learn how to proactively participate in the civic life of the community, state, province, and nation, be open to different perspectives, new ideas, and new ways of thinking, and be able to civilly dialogue with others who have differences in perspective and come from different cultures.

These societal changes and citizenship needs, coupled with updated research and understanding of how people learn, strongly suggest the need for a challenging, high-level education that raises the bar for all students. As indicated in table I.1 (page 4), these changes include, among other things, growth in understanding and complex skill development over time, greater engagement, purposeful learning, active understanding, more complex thinking and problem solving, and more effective collaborative learning. These learning principles and their practical implications, adapted from work originally developed by education author Jay McTighe and Seif (2010), guide the ideas and practices suggested in this book. You can use the reproducible "Learning Principles and Suggestions for Teaching and Learning" (page 14) for your own examination of these ideas.

TABLE I.1: Learning Principles and Education Implications

Principle of Learning	Implications
Meaningful learning is active and engaging.	Students should be actively engaged in the learning process and not be passive recipients of knowledge.
Learning is purposeful and contextual.	Learning should be focused on relevant and interesting questions, significant problems, and meaningful challenges.
Experts organize or chunk their knowledge around transferable core concepts or big ideas.	Learning should be framed around understanding and applying core ideas, not as learning separate, discrete facts and skills.
Learning is mediated and enhanced through different types of thinking.	Students should be engaged in many types of thinking to deepen and apply their learning, such as by classifying and categorizing, reasoning inferentially, analyzing, and thinking creatively.
Understanding is revealed and demonstrated when students can apply, transfer, and adapt their learning to new and novel situations and problems.	Students should have multiple opportunities to apply their learning in meaningful and varied contexts.
New learning is built on and integrated with prior knowledge.	Teachers should help students actively connect new information and ideas to what they already know.
Learning is social.	Students should have multiple opportunities for interactive, collaborative learning in a supportive environment.
Learning is more likely to occur when students have a growth mindset.	Students should have opportunities to be curious, ask questions, take learning risks, and learn from failure. They should often be provided with feedback that helps them improve their work.

Learning is nonlinear; it develops and deepens over time.	Students should be involved in revisiting core ideas and processes so as to develop deeper, more complex, and more sophisticated learning over time.
Learning increases when students are interested in what they are learning.	Teachers should make every effort to find ways to interest students in what they are learning. Where possible, students should be given choices—of courses to take, projects to do, books to read, assessments used to evaluate, and more.

Sources: Bransford, Brown, & Cocking, 1999; Colvin, 2008; Dweck, 2006; Hattie, 2012; McTighe & Seif, 2010; Mehta & Fine, 2019; National Research Council, 2005; Shenk, 2010.

In addition, many of the qualities necessary for future workers and citizens focus not only on cognitive skill development but also around the development of soft skills, including communication and self-management, and critical habits of mind, including persistence and metacognition (Costa & Kallick, 2000, 2008). Employers at Google (as cited in Strauss, 2017) assert that the most important qualities of its top employees include:

> Being a good coach; communicating and listening well; possessing insights into others (including others' different values and points of view); having empathy toward and being supportive of one's colleagues; being a good critical thinker and problem solver; and being able to make connections across complex ideas.

The big surprise was that STEM expertise came in dead last in their list of important skills (Strauss, 2017)! A critical link among these soft skills and habits of mind is the ability to continually relate to and work with others, learn and grow, face challenges, solve problems, and retool in light of a changing economy and society.

I find that the name that best incorporates research-based learning principles and preparing students to adapt to societal changes is *lifelong learning*. There are other names used by other authors who also suggest this type of learning—*deep learning* (Mehta & Fine, 2019) is one, and *learning that lasts* (Berger, Woodfin, & Vilen, 2016) is another. In this book, *deep learning* is only one part of a lifelong learning framework. There are many other ways to create learning that lasts other than the approaches suggested in this book. I use the term *lifelong learning* because it best suggests the type of learning that is needed—relevant, engaging, challenging, and interesting, with a focus on developing, over time, a complex knowledge base, critical skills, growth mindset, and the ability to learn and problem solve independently and interdependently. A lifelong learning education prepares students not only for the present, but also prepares them to be continuous learners who are able to learn and grow and deal with the challenges of a changing and uncertain world.

Education for Lifelong Learning

Education is at a crossroads. On the one hand, many classrooms and schools still provide a traditional educational approach, using a model similar to one that has been around for many years. This approach generally does not encourage or enhance student curiosity or promote a growth mindset. Too few students are enveloped in learning experiences that deepen their understanding of key concepts in subject areas, or raise the level of their thinking, or enable them to create their own interpretations, explanations, and narratives.

For example, Mehta and Fine (2019) find that the typical instructional approach in secondary schools is passive, low-level learning, mostly around textbook reading and assignments, lectures and recitations, and formula plug-ins (mathematics). As they observed in the many high schools that they visited:

> Students who had been chattering excitedly in the hall only a moment before sat stone-faced in class. Students told us over and over that they couldn't see the point of what they were doing, that there was little connection to any real-world application, and that they came to school mainly to see their friends and participate in extracurriculars, or to get to college. (p. 17)

> In classroom after classroom, students were not being challenged to think. Roughly speaking, about four out of five classrooms we visited featured tasks that were in the bottom half of Bloom's taxonomy, asking students to recall, comprehend, or apply, rather than to analyze, synthesize, or create. Another way of putting this: if we stapled ourselves to a student for a day, we likely would encounter one class, or occasionally two, that presented genuine opportunities for critical thinking or analysis. Consistent with prior studies, teacher talk far outran student talk; the modal task for students continues to be to take notes on teacher-delivered content about pre-

> established knowledge. Math tasks continued, on the
> whole, to be algorithmic, asking students to apply exist-
> ing formulas to a series of practice problems. (Mehta &
> Fine, 2019, pp. 24–25)

Another study (Nehring, Charner-Laird, & Szczesiul, 2017) finds that in nine high-performing secondary schools, most teaching tasks require little complex thought and usually focus on recall or simple application; content was sometimes offered "at a blistering pace" (p. 40); only seven of twenty-two classrooms observed had a "depth and breadth of intellectual demand" (p. 41); and typical traditional assessments were "associated with a limited range of skills" (p. 42).

A comment by a former student (as cited in Soots, 2020) sums up many of the problems high school students face as they try to get a rigorous, relevant education:

> I dislike how AP classes prompt students to prioritize passing a test over being intellectually engaged with the course material. For many AP classes, my peers and I worry about getting a 4 or 5 on the exam, rather than retaining what we learn. In my Spanish Literature class this year, we are flying through the long list of texts the course expects us to cover but lacking time to thought-fully focus on each text.

In elementary classrooms, some teachers provide limited opportunities for students to read and think about substantive literature, engage students in meaningful science activities, understand geographic cultures and historical concepts, or analyze the work of great artists. For example, education journalist Natalie Wexler (2019b) explores how the recurrent and repetitive emphasis in elementary schools on low-level skill development, focused almost exclusively around reading and mathematics, fails to provide students with the time and opportunity to develop a solid foundation of content knowledge, understanding, and skills they need for furthering their education and understanding the world around them. Mathematics educator and parent Kathy Liu Sun (2019) expresses concern that elementary mathematics instruction relies heavily on worksheets in the early grades and often focuses on learning procedures and memorizing rules rather than building curiosity about mathematics and encouraging engagement, thinking, and creativity.

In *The Opportunity Myth*, The New Teacher Project (TNTP, n.d.) explains that too many K–12 students are "ill-prepared to live the lives they hope for." In the nearly one thousand observed K–12 classroom lessons:

> Students were working on activities related to class 88 percent of the time and met the demands of their assignments 71 percent of the time . . . Yet students only demonstrated mastery of grade level standards on their assignments . . . 17 percent of the time . . . Students spent more than 500 hours per school year on assignments that weren't appropriate for their grade and with instruction that didn't ask enough of them—the equivalent of six months of wasted class time in each core subject. (TNTP, n.d.)

TNTP (2019) summarizes the results of this study this way:

> Across the five school systems we studied . . . we found that an average student spent almost three-quarters of their time . . . on assignments that were not grade-appropriate. In a single school year, that's the equivalent of more than six months of learning time.

> We met eighth graders in an ELA classroom who were asked to fill in missing vowels in a vocabulary worksheet, and students in an AP physics classroom who spent an entire class period making a vocabulary poster. These sound like extreme examples, but they were far more the norm than the exception.

About This Book

This book is designed to help teachers examine, understand, adopt, and put into practice the goals of a lifelong learning education by raising students' level of learning, engaging them, and preparing them for our changing world. Another way to think about this book is that it suggests how to create *lifeworthy learning*—learning that is more central to students' lives now and in their futures (Perkins, 2014).

Chapters 1 through 4 describe and explain the teaching goals, instructional framework, assessment approaches, and curriculum characteristics of a lifelong learning education. Chapter 5 examines two additional areas that help a teacher implement a lifelong learning education—project-based learning and civics education. Chapter 6 suggests how educators can plan their implementation of a lifelong learning education. Table I.2 outlines the book's key questions and big ideas by chapter.

TABLE I.2: Moving Teaching Toward Lifelong Learning–
Key Ideas

Key Questions	Big Ideas
Chapter 1: What are the key teaching goals for a lifelong learning education program? What should students accomplish to prepare them for the future?	Educators adopt four key learning goals so that students do the following. 1. Develop a growth mindset. 2. Build a foundation of key knowledge, understandings, and skills. 3. Deepen learning. 4. Broaden and enrich their learning.

Chapter 2: How do we rethink instruction in order to develop a lifelong learning educational program?	Revolve instruction around the following.
	 • Active, engaging learning strategies and activities
	 • A four-phase instructional model as follows.
	  1. Setting the stage
	  2. Building the foundation
	  3. Deepening learning
	  4. Providing closure

Chapter 3: How do we refocus assessments in order to develop a lifelong learning education program?	Reframe assessment around the following. • Diagnostic, formative, and summative assessments designed to raise the level of and improve student learning and student work • Core lifelong learning assessments • Portfolios that tell a more complete story of how well students are learning and growing
Chapter 4: How do we adapt the curriculum in order to develop a lifelong education program?	• Use twelve lifelong learning education criteria to analyze the current curriculum or adopt new curricula. • Redesign the curriculum using the Understanding by Design curriculum framework (Wiggins & McTighe, 2011).

continued →

Chapter 5: What is the relationship between lifelong learning education, project-based learning, and civics education?	Examine why and how it is important to incorporate learning that includes the following. • Project-based learning • A coherent, comprehensive civics education program
Chapter 6: How can teachers and schools plan for and implement a lifelong learning education?	• Use four research-based principles of effective organizational change to help implement a lifelong learning education. • Use the four-phase instructional model to plan for and implement lifelong learning education changes.

At the end of each chapter, I include some websites that can be helpful in developing a lifelong learning education school program by improving educational goals, instruction, assessment, curriculum, and more. Please note that the specific technology or internet examples integrated into the book and online are, as of this writing, available and live, but due to the evolving nature of technology, that may change in the future. Following the technology resources in each chapter, I suggest reproducible activities that are designed to help you reflect on and synthesize key ideas, and propose action steps that can help you apply the ideas to teaching and learning.

A more exhaustive list of lifelong learning technology resources, located at **go .SolutionTree.com/21stcenturyskills**, provides many more examples of specific websites, blogs, podcasts, and other technological supports. Online you can find many books, articles, podcasts, and similar resources that can help you better understand the goals and practices of a lifelong learning education, as well as how to implement the different aspects. Many are in the references identified throughout this book (page 189).

Finally, each chapter ends with reproducible "Reflections" and "Action Steps" about that specific content. Begin with the reproducible "Reflections—Introduction" (page 12) and "Action Steps—Introduction" (page 13).

My Hope for This Book

My goal in writing this book is to help teachers better prepare students for a complex, changing world, and to make the purpose and nature of a lifelong learning education clearer, more understandable, more doable, and more practical. My hope is that the book will not only provide some answers for the future of education, but also raise some significant questions in the minds of readers, among them the following.

- What should educators' goals be?

- How do we develop a growth mindset in students?

- What are the most important, meaningful foundational knowledge and skills for students?

- What does it mean to deepen, enrich, and broaden student learning?

- What specific types of instruction and assessments are best suited for a lifelong learning education?

- What types of curricula are most conducive to educating students for lifelong learning?

- How do educators engage students and help them prepare for the world in which they will live, work, and be citizens?

If the book helps to both raise and answer these questions, inspires you to begin to think about and apply aspects of teaching and learning in a new and different way, and helps you consider how to journey along a path toward a lifelong learning education for children, then it will have been successful.

Reflections—Introduction

The following questions and activities should provoke and stimulate thought and discussion about the lifelong learning ideas in this introductory chapter.

- Review the video game learning description at the beginning of this introduction. How might this type of learning be adapted to educational practice? Write your own description of a classroom, school, or district that develops more complex, expert learners over time.

- Review the reasons for moving toward a lifelong learning education examined in this introduction, which are as follows.

    ◇ Changes to the nature of work

    ◇ Changes to technology and its effects on society

    ◇ Rapidity of change

    ◇ Research on learning principles

Action Steps—Introduction

The following suggests initial actions that you might take to adopt and implement rigorous learning.

- Review the research-based principles in table I.1 (page 4). How consistent are these principles with your own best, most powerful learning experiences? In the reproducible "Learning Principles and Suggestions for Teaching and Learning" (page 14), based on a review of the principles, consider how each principle is or is not consistent with your own best learning experiences and suggest ways that you can make your own teaching and learning more consistent with the learning principles.

- Table I.2 (page 9) illustrates the big ideas from each chapter. To prepare for the rest of the book, think about the implications of these ideas for teaching goals, classroom instruction, assessment, and curriculum. Jot down three to five practical implications and changes to teaching and learning that might result from these big ideas. Be prepared to compare your ideas with the information gleaned from the remaining chapters in the book.

- This introduction argues that a rapidly changing society requires a new educational vision for college, career, and citizenship preparation. Based on these changes, make a list of five to ten recommended adjustments that you would make to teaching and learning. Using these recommended adjustments, create a persuasive essay with arguments and evidence for implementing these suggestions. Be prepared to share and discuss your essay with others.

Learning Principles and Suggestions for Teaching and Learning

Based on a review of the learning principles listed in the following table and a comparison with your own experiences, make a list of practical action steps that you can take to make teaching and learning more consistent with these learning principles.

Principle of Learning	How Consistent Is This Principle With My Best Learning Experiences?	Suggestions for Teaching and Learning
Meaningful learning is active and engaging.		
Learning is purposeful and contextual.		
Experts organize or chunk their knowledge around transferable core concepts or big ideas.		
Learning is mediated and enhanced through different types of thinking.		
Understanding is revealed and demonstrated when students can apply, transfer, and adapt their learning to new and novel situations and problems.		

page 1 of 2

Teaching for Lifelong Learning © 2021 Elliott Seif • SolutionTree.com
Visit **go.SolutionTree.com/21stcenturyskills** to download this free reproducible.

New learning is built on and integrated with prior knowledge.		
Learning is social.		
Learning is more likely to occur when students have a growth mindset.		
Learning is nonlinear; it develops and deepens over time.		
Learning increases when students are interested in what they are learning.		

Source: Adapted from McTighe, J., & Seif, E. (2010). An implementation framework to support 21st century skills. In J. Bellanca & R. Brandt (Eds.), 21st century skills: Rethinking how students learn *(pp. 149–172). Bloomington, IN: Solution Tree Press.*

Teaching for Lifelong Learning © 2021 Elliott Seif • SolutionTree.com
Visit **go.SolutionTree.com/21stcenturyskills** to download this free reproducible.

CHAPTER 1

Understanding Educator Goals That Support Students' Lifelong Learning

Without some goals and some efforts to reach it, no man can live.

—John Dewey

n this chapter, you will examine four key goals that support a lifelong learning education.

1. **Develop a growth mindset** so that students are interested in learning, motivated to find answers, engaged in exploring ideas, and know how to improve their learning and their work over time.

2. **Build a foundation** of key understandings and skills that are relevant, meaningful, and significant.

3. **Deepen learning and develop independent learners** as they research and inquire, using their foundational understandings and skills to examine and analyze thoughtful challenges, debate issues, perceptively understand diverse ideas, and pursue their interests.

4. **Broaden and enrich experiences** to help students discover and develop their talents, strengths, and interests; provide opportunities to have authentic experiences and try new things; and deepen their interests through apprenticeships, community activism, service learning opportunities, and the like.

Two Different Learning Examples

As indicated in the introduction, how people learn and the challenges of teaching and learning in a changing world suggest that we need to engage students more actively in the learning process, raise the level and types of thinking students do in classrooms, and in general make learning more rigorous and relevant. This is a critical challenge for educators. But in many classrooms, it's often not clear as to what it means to prepare students for a lifetime of learning.

In order to identify the key goals of a lifelong learning education, and to illustrate how they might be put into practice, two different scenarios are presented. These scenarios teach the same topic—the study of explorers—in a fifth-grade classroom, but from two very different perspectives. The first example typifies what researchers call *didactic*, or teacher-centered, instruction (Smith, Lee, & Newmann, 2001). The second example is typical of the *interactive* method of instruction.

Scenario One

In this fifth-grade lesson on early explorers of the New World, the teacher first puts the following student objectives on the board and reads them to students.

> *At the end of this unit, you will be able to:*
> * *Define vocabulary words associated with early New World explorers*
> * *Recall the names of famous New World explorers and their destinations*
> * *Locate the explorers' starting points and travel routes on a map*
> * *Identify two reasons for the exploration of the New World*
> * *Improve your skill in finding the main ideas from a reading*

The students then take turns reading aloud from the textbook, and as they read, the teacher defines new words on the board and lists the names of explorers and their destinations. She stops the reading to point out a map in the text that identifies the starting points, travel routes, and ending locations of the explorers. She asks students to spend ten minutes quietly and individually studying the map, and then to select and be prepared to share a main idea about the explorers that they gleaned from the map. She calls on some students to share their main ideas, which she also writes on the board.

The teacher asks students to work in pairs and complete a crossword puzzle built from the explorer vocabulary words in the text. At the end of the unit, each student gets a worksheet handout that has a set of questions asking about explorer vocabulary terms, the names of famous explorers, and explorer destinations. Students examine a list of question responses placed at the bottom of the worksheet, and then write what they think is the correct response under each question. The class gets thirty minutes to complete this exercise.

Scenario Two

In the classroom next door, another fifth-grade teacher is taking a different approach to the unit on explorers. The teacher has derived a few key concepts from the goals of the unit—the meaning of exploration, the difficulties faced by explorers, the rules and rewards of exploration, and the risks of exploration—and from them developed a few key essential questions that "focus the unit and prioritize learning" (Wiggins & McTighe, 2011, p. 70).

In her introduction to the fifth-grade unit on early explorers, she uses the following essential questions.

- Why do people explore?

- What must explorers endure?

- What are the risks and rewards of exploration?

- Why do explorers take so many risks?

To stimulate students' interest and curiosity about what they will learn, the teacher introduces these questions to students, defines new terms found in the questions (for example, *endure*, *risks*, and *rewards*), and gives students a chance to think about and share what they already know about each question before they begin studying New World explorers. As students learn more about the explorers who traditionally have been credited with finding the territory that would become the United States of America, they will reexamine the essential questions to consider how unit activities answer the questions and further discuss and clarify the answers.

Next, the teacher and students together read from a text about the early New World explorers. As students read, they use the survey, question, read, recite, and review (SQ3R) study method (Robinson, 1946). They first *survey* the text for information that might help answer the essential questions, and then develop additional *questions* from the text headings. Then, as they go back and *read* the text more carefully, they are asked to pick out key ideas and state (*recite*) these ideas to a partner. Finally, the teacher and students together write a *review* of what they have learned so far as answers to both the essential questions and the SQ3R questions, and further discuss and develop explorer vocabulary and concepts.

In another lesson, in small groups, students are tasked with creating timeline maps that show for each major explorer the years exploration took place, where the explorers started from, what routes they took, miles and days they traveled, where they landed, and any additional helpful information. As students complete this activity, they collect additional information from their text and use computers to research information from other sources. They draw conclusions from this information by discussing what their results tell them about these explorers, the difficulties they faced, the risks they took, and what else they discovered. When they complete the timeline maps, students hang them around the classroom and do a gallery walk (walking around the classroom in small groups) to examine all the timeline maps their peers completed for this activity.

Using the data collected in the last activity, the entire class, working together with the teacher's guidance, develops a chart that compares and contrasts key information for each explorer. Students are given the opportunity to examine and write about the similarities and differences between these explorers. The teacher then divides students into small groups again. Each group is assigned one explorer and conducts further research on that explorer, finding additional articles and readings, and adding to the information and understanding already gleaned from their work so far. Emphasis is on increasing knowledge and understanding of the explorers' goals, what they wanted to achieve, the challenges they faced, the risks they took, the hardships they endured and overcame, what they discovered, and what they accomplished. Each group shares their results using their own display chart.

For the final assessment, students answer the following questions in a short essay, with their resources available to them, and then discuss their answers first in small groups and then together with the entire class.

- Which explorer that we have studied is the most interesting? Why?
- Which explorer faced the most hardships? Took the most risks? How did he overcome his hardships and risks?
- Which explorer was the most important? Why?
- What have you learned about exploration that is important for understanding explorers in the modern world?

Lifelong Learning Goals

After reading both of these teaching scenarios, consider the following questions: What are the differences in the goals and instructional characteristics between these two examples? Why is the latter an example of a lifelong learning approach?

Here is my analysis: in the first scenario, students develop a very limited understanding of the explorers and why they came to America. The learning seems somewhat random, built around arbitrary factual information. There is no focus on meaningful questions or ideas. For example, many options for meaningful learning about explorers exist. Students could learn about the role of explorers then and now, understand how geography affects exploration, analyze the similarities among and differences between explorers, examine the hardships and challenges they faced, understand the clash of cultures and its consequences, or consider the overall consequences of the explorers' actions. However, none of these topics or themes are developed. While some basic knowledge is learned, much of it will probably be forgotten, since there is little studied that is relevant to students, no connections are made to previous learning, and there is little if any activity designed to help students remember and apply what they have learned.

This teacher also fails to incorporate the learning and practice of key learning to learn skills, such as defining problems and challenges, conducting research, thinking, and writing. There are no opportunities for students to ask their own questions about explorers and exploration, define the problems and challenges facing explorers, search for and process information about explorers on their own, sort and classify information and data, develop causal patterns, compare and contrast, interpret events, or write coherent essays or self-reflections.

Finally, this teacher praises quiet and orderly behavior, and is the center of learning. She rarely engages the class in substantive conversation. There is very limited student engagement and involvement. There is no effort to stimulate student curiosity about explorers or exploration. Students are not encouraged to learn more about explorers or exploration on their own.

Careful examination and analysis of the second example indicates that the teacher does things very differently from the first teacher. She incorporates the following four lifelong learning education goals into her teaching and learning strategies.

- Developing a growth mindset in students
- Building a foundation of key understandings and skills

- Deepening learning and developing independent learners
- Broadening and enriching experiences

Goal One: Developing a Growth Mindset in Students

In scenario two, the teacher creates many activities that foster curiosity and a growth mindset. According to Dweck (2006, 2015), people with a growth mindset see themselves as learners who thrive on new challenges. They believe that their intelligence and skills are flexible, and they can get better at what they are able to do and understand by accepting challenges, persisting in the face of difficulties, practicing in ways that improve their learning, and finding others to provide help when needed. This is in contrast to people who have a mostly fixed mindset (because everyone has some of each), believing that intelligence is an innate feature that can't be improved, leading to giving up when faced with challenges (Dweck, 2006, 2015).

Dweck (2006) describes six key indicators of a growth mindset.

1. Feeling positive about and accepting new challenges
2. Believing that basic skills, intelligence, and talents can be improved through effort, hard work, practice, and working through difficulties
3. Believing that setbacks and failures provide learning opportunities
4. Being comfortable finding help and support when needed
5. Looking for models and examples of success and good work
6. Striving to improve and do better

Curiosity

Another key indicator of a growth mindset is curiosity. With a "culture of inquisitiveness" (Barell, 2003, p. 1), teachers foster interest and motivate students to find answers, encourage them to explore ideas, and develop meaningful, authentic tasks. Research supports that curiosity is a major factor in positive and long-lasting learning experiences and high achievement. In a classic study, mental health professionals Adam Grant and Allison Sweet Grant (2020) found that world-class artists, athletes, musicians, and scientists typically had an early coach or teacher who made learning fun and motivated them to hone their skills. An analysis of 125 studies of nearly 200,000 students found that the more the students enjoyed learning and were encouraged to be curious, the better they performed, from elementary school all the way through college. Students with high levels of intellectual curiosity get better grades than their peers, even after controlling for their intelligence quotient and work ethic.

Unfortunately, as in the first explorer scenario (page 18), many teachers lessen student curiosity and interest by introducing a unit with a set of very specific objectives and then moving quickly through lessons and content to reach these objectives. However, in a lifelong learning approach, an important challenge is to create learning experiences that engage students and develop *curious explorers* who are interested in what they are studying and learning.

Essential Questions

In scenario two of the explorer unit, one specific way that the teacher tries to heighten curiosity and interest in the explorer topic is by centering the unit study around a few focused, relevant, interesting questions, called *essential questions* (McTighe & Wiggins, 2013; Wiggins & McTighe, 2005). That teacher's essential questions follow.

- Why do people explore?

- What must they endure?

- What are the risks and rewards?

- Why do they take so many risks?

Centering a unit around essential questions like these, designed to interest students in discovering more about what is being studied, is helpful in developing curious explorers in virtually any subject. These kinds of questions have "emotive force with an intellectual bite, and readily invite the exploration of ideas" (Wilson, 2014).

For example, here are some key learning goals for biology courses and units, expressed in terms of essential questions, that can be adapted to any biology unit, K–12.

- What are the differences between living and nonliving things? What does it mean to be alive?

- How do organisms live and grow? How do they survive?

- How are the traits of one generation of a living thing passed to the next?

- Why do individuals of the same species and even siblings have different characteristics?

- How do we know that different species are related?

- How do organisms interact with each other? What are helpful and harmful types of interactions?

- How and why do organisms interact with their environment, and what are the positive and negative effects of those interactions?

Consider how these essential questions might influence the way students think about learning biology. How could an educator use them to introduce biology units of study? How would they create greater curiosity about and motivation for what is to come?

What are some of the major characteristics of good essential questions? In their book on essential questions, Understanding by Design creators Jay McTighe and Grant Wiggins (2013) propose three major characteristics.

1. Essential questions are important and timeless. They "arise naturally and recur throughout one's life. Such questions are broad in scope and universal by nature . . . [They] are common and perpetually arguable" (pp. 5–6). Questions such as, What is ethical behavior?, What does it mean to live a good life?, What is progress?, and What is beauty? are examples of important and timeless questions.

2. Essential questions focus learning around key ideas in a discipline. These questions focus on a subject's big ideas "to the frontiers of technical knowledge. They are historically important" and relevant (p. 6). Examples include, How do scientists discover truth?, What is good art?, What is poetry?, How can we interpret the writing of this specific author?, and How do historians develop historical interpretations?

3. Essential questions are vital or necessary for personal understanding. These questions help "students make sense of seemingly isolated facts and skills or important but abstract ideas and strategies" (McTighe & Wiggins, 2013, p. 6). For example, when someone is beginning to learn chess, the person sees good chess players seemingly make random moves on the chessboard. The person learning might ask him- or herself, "How can I make sense of these moves? What patterns and insights can help me understand strategies that work in a chess game?" Similarly, a student might read a book with seemingly isolated facts and information about characters and a random plot, and ask, "How can I interpret, analyze, and make sense of the information and ideas in this book?"

These three key characteristics, taken together, do the following.

- **Require broad understanding:** There is no simple right answer. The question is not built around one or even a few facts.

- **Raise important ideas at the heart of a discipline:** The question supports inquiry into important concepts and ideas that are or have been debated and discussed in the discipline.

- **Raise important personal questions or interdisciplinary ideas:** The question focuses on making sense of important ideas that help students make sense out of their learning or cuts across several disciplines, such as questions about climate change, war and peace, the effects of technological changes, or moral issues.

- **Provoke and stimulate thinking:** The question is open to discussion, interpretation, analysis, and creativity.

- **May recur:** The question may also be relevant and useful for studying other topics and units both within the subject and within other subjects as well.

Figure 1.1 provides sample essential questions by subject that teachers can adapt to many different grade levels.

History
• What makes someone American (or Canadian, Nigerian, or Peruvian, for example), and why? How has the answer to this question changed over time?
• Who are some of the heroes of history, and what makes them so?

Science
• How do animals adapt to their environments in order to survive? When have humans shown this kind of adaptation?
• What does it mean to be alive?
• How do we maintain and support life?
• What makes a lab or study result reliable? How do you decide?

Reading and Writing
• What literature is worth reading, and what makes it so?
• What is the moral of the story?
• How do you organize writing so that it becomes worth reading?

Figure 1.1: Sample essential questions by subject.   continued →

Mathematics
• What types of problems and challenges does this mathematical way of thinking help us solve?
• How does this mathematical way of thinking help us to solve problems more efficiently and effectively?

World Languages and Cultures
• What is culture?
• How are daily lives and traditions in other countries and cultures similar to and different from mine?
• How do languages shape a worldview?

Visual and Performing Arts
• What is "good" art, and how do we know?
• How can we interpret a play (or a piece of art or a dance number, for example)?
• How does art impact science or history, and how does science or history impact art?

Health and Physical Education
• How do you maintain a healthy body and mind?
• What is wellness? How has the perception of wellness changed over time, and how does this perception impact our understanding of wellness now?
• What strategies and skills enable me to play the game well?

Career and Technical Education
• How do I work together with others to improve the health of members of our community?
• How do I create food that is both delicious and nutritious?
• How do I develop an understanding of auto repair techniques and strategies that support the safety and well-being of drivers and passengers?
• How can those who work in the tourism industry provide their guests with superior service?

Goal Two: Building a Foundation of Key Understandings and Skills

In the second explorer unit, the teacher's objectives include enabling students to build a vocabulary of core concepts, broaden their understanding of exploration, and create a web of facts and ideas that demonstrates a complexity of understanding. The teacher is also helping students to learn and practice important skills, such as comprehension, writing, research, thinking, and collaborating with others. In other words, this second unit is much better designed to create a rich foundation of under-standings, associated background knowledge, and critical skills.

If educators want to create a lifelong learning program that, over time, develops and refines complex ideas and teaches students critical skills, they will need to define a core foundation of knowledge and understandings, as well as develop ways of enabling students to continually learn and practice critical skills (Willingham, 2019). All educators should consider the following questions.

- What are the most important and meaningful concepts, knowledge, ideas, and understandings we want students to learn and build on?

- What are the most important skills we want students to practice and be able to perform well?

Answering these two questions is the best way to design a modern, rigorous school program with a focus on big ideas and core skills that support lifelong learning.

Identifying Core Content

How do you determine what are the most important and meaningful concepts, knowledge, ideas, and understandings students should learn in any subject or grade level? Let's start with an example. Suppose we try to identify the most meaningful and important foundational ideas that we want students to learn and focus on as they study U.S. history. What might those foundational ideas be? The following list has thirteen key ideas, some or all of which might be central to the study of American history at any grade level.

1. America's principles of democracy were forged by founders in the writing of the Declaration of Independence and the Constitution. The same founders also created processes for interpreting and adapting the law over time, including how to amend the Constitution.

2. The role of government at all levels is and has been a source of conflict and debate throughout American history.

3. America's geography has been a key factor in determining its history. The interaction between the environment and American society has been a major factor in American life.

4. Immigration from all over the world has been a source of both strength and conflict throughout American history.

5. Throughout American history there has been a continual clash between the forces for continuity (tradition) and the forces for change.

6. Four of America's key values include (1) a pioneering spirit,
    (2) entrepreneurship, (3) innovation, and (4) pragmatism.

7. The struggle for human and civil rights for all is a constant theme
    throughout American history.

8. America's economy is built around market-based capitalism and has
    changed dramatically many times.

9. America has seen, and continues to see, a continual clash of ideas that
    has led to both violent and peaceful conflict.

10. Throughout American history, many individuals and groups have had
    a major, positive influence on American society.

11. Science, technology, and religion have been driving forces in
    American society.

12. The concept of the American dream has been a driving force for
    Americans and the world.

13. Foreign policy evolves continually and often vacillates between
    isolationism and global leadership.

These thirteen big ideas (or ideas like these) and essential questions tied to them can form the nexus of foundational understandings in American history. The study of American history at any level might stress one or more of these ideas as its primary learning goal. For example, a second-grade class might use many children's books to study individuals who made a difference in American history (key idea number 10). Young students can also learn about the geography of their community and how it affects the way they live (key idea number 3). A middle school unit built around the study of the American Revolution might focus on the very idea of government and what it is supposed to represent to its people. The unit could include exploring the conflict over the role of government, the differences between monarchy, republic, and democracy, and taxation without representation (key idea numbers 9 and 10).

A high school American history unit might focus on how the Constitution was developed and its outcome (key idea numbers 1 and 2). Another high school unit on the Great Depression could focus on the question of whether it was a good idea for the federal government to pass laws to try to end the Depression. This unit might stress the causes of the Depression and the principles of a market-based economy, include a discussion of the conflicting ideas about interjecting government programs into the marketplace, and explore the key outcomes of the government's role during the Depression (key idea numbers 2, 5, and 8).

Through the teaching of the American history course at all levels, students might learn about immigrants who came from other parts of the world and whose descendants live in local communities, or research the waves of immigration and the individuals and groups that have made a difference in American life (key idea number 4). Some periods in American history, such as the period of industrialization, could focus on dynamic technological change (key idea number 11), while others (for example, colonial America) might focus on geography and the environment (key idea number 3). The questions, What is the American dream? and Does it still exist? (key idea number 12) might become the key essential questions for an entire American history course.

Here's another example: a set of central ideas for teaching biology, developed in conjunction with the essential biology questions described earlier (page 23). Consider how a teacher might adapt these central ideas in order to make them the focus of biology units and courses, K–12, and how the teacher might introduce these ideas alongside the essential questions.

- Organisms share common characteristics of life.
- Cells have organized structures and systems needed to maintain life.
- Structure is related to function at all biological levels of organization.
- Through a variety of mechanisms, organisms seek to maintain a biological balance between internal and external environments.
- Organisms obtain and use energy to carry out life processes.
- Genetic information is inherited and expressed.
- Evolution is the result of many random processes selected for the survival and reproduction of a population.
- Organisms on earth interact with and depend in various ways on other living and nonliving things in their environments.
- Over time, through scientific inquiry and investigation, biologists and others have discovered, refined, and continue to discover and refine the key knowledge, theories, and principles of biology.

These two examples illustrate how, through the analysis of standards, texts, and other sources, it is possible to narrow down and identify the underlying, foundational knowledge, understandings, and questions that will provide a central focus for what students must learn in different units and courses at all levels, K–12.

Identifying Foundational Skills

What are the most important skills that students should practice and be able to perform well in any subject and at any grade level? In addition to core content, teaching for lifelong learning also prioritizes skills that students will use throughout their lives.

Standards and other appropriate resources can help teachers determine which skills should become priorities. For example, the *American Association of School Librarians for Learners* (American Association of School Librarians, 2018), a very valuable source of skill standards, indicates that students need to know how to formulate questions and use evidence to investigate questions, identify a variety of sources, assess the validity and accuracy of information, and reflect on its quality and usefulness. Unpacking and prioritizing standards are the focus of many books, including *Understanding by Design* (Wiggins & McTighe, 2005) and *Design in Five: Essential Phases to Create Engaging Assessment Practice* (Dimich, 2014).

As a result of my own analysis of many standards and other educational resources, I have identified six critical skill sets (and their components) as the major skills focus for a lifelong learning educational foundation. Table 1.1 lists them.

TABLE 1.1: Foundational Skill Sets

Develop understanding
Students are able to:
• Discern patterns and build relationships among information and data (for example, story narratives, cause-and-effect timelines)
• Summarize and explain ideas, concepts, theories, principles, and hypotheses
• Develop concepts by sorting and categorizing information and data
• Find similarities and differences, compare and contrast
• Interpret and form theories, and examine and explain the evidence that supports them
Conduct research
Students are able to:
• Search for, read, and comprehend many different types of texts
• Find and evaluate information, ideas, and data
• Sort through, find, summarize, and evaluate the most useful information
• Determine the most reliable and valid information and data

Think critically and creatively

Students are able to:

- Analyze, interpret, and draw conclusions from information and data
- Symbolically represent information and quantitative data in graphic formats
- Summarize and synthesize information and ideas
- Think logically and draw conclusions from logic
- Think inductively: observe, make inferences, generate hypotheses, create experiments, test, and rethink
- Form opinions backed by argument and evidence
- Solve complex problems
- Creatively solve problems by rethinking questions, brainstorming alternatives, creating solutions, and planning for implementation

Communicate effectively

Students are able to:

- Describe and explain ideas and demonstrate understanding either orally or in writing
- Write narratives, stories, research papers, op-ed pieces, letters to the editor, and so on
- Represent and share data and ideas in many different formats
- Participate in discussions effectively
- Develop, share, and discuss persuasive arguments with claims and evidence
- Create and share oral and written presentations

Collaborate

Students are able to:

- Have and show empathy and support colleagues
- Coach others
- Communicate clearly and listen to others
- Collaborate and problem solve as they conduct research, think critically and creatively, and complete projects

Apply and transfer learning to new situations

Students are able to:

- Use what they have learned in different settings and situations to demonstrate understanding
- Grasp concepts, principles, or skills to apply to new problems and situations

Sources for standards: National Council for the Social Studies, 2010; NGSS Lead States, 2013; Sources: Adapted from Conley, 2010; Wagner, 2014.

The development and growth of these foundational skills should be ongoing, integrated into the learning process, and taught frequently as a regular part of the school experience at each level. Students should learn and practice these skills, become better at doing them, and build the complexity necessary to use them effectively. For example, the development of research skills can begin with simple tasks at the early childhood and elementary levels (such as finding information about an author or searching for information about how specific plants survive) and advance into more complex research tasks (including writing a research paper) as students progress into middle and high school. Foundational skills are most likely to be included as part of an ongoing curriculum if teachers see their importance and make learning and improving them a priority (Schmoker, 2018).

Goal Three: Deepening Learning and Developing Independent Learners

Goal two focuses on the need for developing a foundation of knowledge and understanding and acquiring skills that are the basics of lifelong learning. This goal—deepening learning and developing independent learners—goes beyond foundational learning. In order to better understand the difference between foundational and deep learning, consider how people learn statistics or to play a sport. Developing a foundation of understandings and skills is necessary for deep learning in both these areas (Willingham, 2019). In statistics, such a foundation includes understanding basic mathematical functions, such as addition and subtraction and basic statistical terms and functions, such as mean, median, and mode. In learning to play a sport, the foundation is learning the basic rules of the game and the basic skills and strategies of a sport. In learning a musical instrument, foundational learning includes being able to read music and understanding key signatures, tempo signs, music composition, and chord structure.

Sports coaches build a strong foundation in their players through guided skill and teamwork practice as well as scrimmages. Music teachers guide their students as they develop and maintain an interest in music, practice performance skills, and learn music theory. Then, in both music and sports, there is a tipping point (Gladwell, 2000) when players or performers have developed enough of a foundation that they are able to independently or interdependently continue to learn and build on their foundational knowledge and skills. Students transition into deep learning by using and applying their foundational knowledge, skills, and habits of mind (for example, to perform more difficult pieces of music and interpret music on their own—still with guidance—or to adapt complex sports plays for specific situations by operating more independently and flexibly than in the foundation stage). Students may also independently share their musical abilities with others or share their knowledge and skills on how to play a game. In other words, they impart knowledge, understanding, and skills. They become teachers.

Educational psychologist Benjamin S. Bloom (1986) called this increasing ability to apply their learning on their own the development of *automaticity*: the "ability to perform [a skill] unconsciously with speed and accuracy while consciously carrying on other brain functions" (p. 70). When someone reaches the tipping point toward automaticity, there is an independent quality to continued learning that is different from the learning that takes place in the foundational stage.

Deep learning means that students are able to spend their time independently or collaboratively using and applying their basic knowledge, understanding, and skills with little or no help or support. They know how to improve their learning on their own and to seek and learn from coaching help when needed. They build on and take their background understanding and skills to new and deeper levels of understanding, competence, thoughtfulness, complexity, engagement, creativity, and independence.

In the redesigned explorer unit (page 19), deeper, independent learning occurs when students further research the life of one explorer. With only minimal support and help from the teacher, students look up information about their explorer and take their own notes, summarize what they have learned, and develop a presentation to share their results in a visual way. Because they have already acquired the requisite knowledge and skills for students at this grade level, this unit affords an expanded opportunity to conduct research, find new information, synthesize results, and communicate what they have learned.

Goal Four: Broadening and Enriching Experiences

Given the bewildering array of options and choices confronting each individual, students also need to broaden and enrich their experiences in order to understand the wider world, and to understand the choices, options, and variety that exist in the outside world. One way to do this is to develop many classroom activities that allow for student choices and options during the learning process. Education author Mike Anderson (2016) says that student choice is more relevant and important than ever because of the following reason:

> As students come to us with increasingly complex needs and abilities, they need diverse and personally relevant opportunities to learn and practice skills and content. When students leave school they will enter a world where

> self-motivation, creativity, autonomy, and perseverance
> are all critically important, and these are characteris-
> tics that are hard to practice in an environment centered
> on standardization and compliance. When students have
> more choice about their learning, they can both find ways
> of learning that match their personal needs and engage
> with work more powerfully, building skills and work habits
> that will serve them well as lifelong learners. (p. 3)

Some examples of choices and options include the following.

Reading Choices

Giving students reading choices and options is an important way to build curiosity about and interest in reading. A classroom activity that promotes students' choosing their own reading selections, *Sustained Silent Reading* (SSR; Garan & Devoogd, 2008), or the innovative *Scaffolded Silent Reading* (ScSR; Reutzel, Jones, Fawson, & Smith, 2008) sets time aside in classrooms and schools for students to silently read a book of their choice. In the traditional SSR experience, an entire class of students, or even an entire school or district, sets aside a time period during which everyone reads something of their choice. A school or district's use of SSR may include everyone in the school—students, teachers, administrators, parent volunteers, and even other school staff, such as custodians and cafeteria workers. There is no requirement as to what kind of book to choose and no requirement related to what happens after the reading occurs. Students do not have to write book reports or share their reading experiences, although in some SSR experiences they may volunteer to talk about their book to interest others in what they read. In the modified version of ScSR, students choose their own reading materials, but also are "held accountable for reading widely across selected literary genres, setting personal goals for completing the reading of books within a timeframe, conferring with their teacher, and completing response projects to share the books they read with others" (Reutzel et al., 2008, p. 196).

Some teachers make reading choices the heart of their school program. Corrina Reamer, an eleventh-grade English teacher at T.C. Williams High School International Academy in Alexandria, Virginia, has developed a classroom library collection of almost one thousand books paid for through online fundraisers and grants. She works with her students throughout the year to find out about their interests and backgrounds and select books that she thinks will greatly interest them. As a result, many of her students have become avid readers and have, on average, achieved two years' worth of reading progress each year (Natanson, 2020).

Unit and Theme Options

Educators can give students choices in the classroom curriculum. For example, as one component of a unit on the American Revolution, students might choose a project that interests them, such as researching a person who was involved in the war or researching an event that happened during it. Teachers might also give students a choice of three possible questions to respond to for a final exam; they have to answer one of the three questions on the test. Teachers also can give students the three questions in advance of the test, so that students can prepare for the question they choose to answer.

Enrichment Options

You can enable students to participate in a variety of enrichment options, both inside and outside the classroom, that helps them expand and discover their interests, talents, strengths, and goals. The wide variety of options might include the following.

- Taking field trips to museums, zoos, supermarkets, small locally owned businesses, or factories
- Learning to play a musical instrument and joining an orchestra
- Playing board games, including chess
- Singing in a choir
- Getting involved in an academic competition
- Starting or joining an interest club
- Pursuing a passion project (see page 36)
- Traveling to a foreign country or communicating consistently with others from foreign countries
- Interviewing people outside the school or members of the local community for a research project
- Apprenticing for a local employer

Many classrooms and schools have created a wide variety of enrichment activities and options for students, but unfortunately too many have limited options. The school differences can be stark. In one high school in suburban Philadelphia that I worked in, teachers created many classroom options for students, and students had more than fifty after-school and in-school options. However, in many urban schools in Philadelphia that I have visited, both classroom and after-school choices and options were very limited.

Passion Projects

Passion projects are student-designed projects built around a student's interest. They allow students to study topics or subjects of interest individually or in groups. This strategy increases "student passion in the classroom and allows students to learn and study independently" (Lester, 2016, p. 2). The projects can revolve around a theme, book, or hobby. They can be part of the classroom or school experience at any level or used as a capstone graduation project. Students can work through the same four phases of instruction while developing the project, but the student does most of the work with help and guidance from the instructor. Passion projects and project-based learning will be further examined in chapter 5 (page 137).

As a practice, complete the reproducible "Goals, Experiences, and Suggestions" (page 39) and identify some of your own educational experiences.

Helpful Websites

Many websites are available to educators who wish to further explore and better understand lifelong learning education goals.

- Coalition of Essential Schools at **www.essentialschools.org**
- Expeditionary Learning Education at **https://eleducation.org**
- Jay McTighe and Associates Consulting at **https://jaymctighe.com**

Visit **go.SolutionTree.com/21stcenturyskills** for live links to these and other resources.

Reflections—Chapter 1

The following questions and activities should provoke and stimulate thought and discussion about lifelong learning goals.

- How we teach and what students learn are determined in large measure by what goals we have for our students. A lifelong learning education approach develops from the set of four goals described in this chapter. Create a visual organizer of the four key lifelong learning goals and their definitions and descriptions. For example, if you start with a tree diagram and put the four goals as the roots, how would you organize the key components of each goal area on the rest of the tree (trunk, branches, leaves, and so on)? Design the organizer to include the key ideas in this chapter and their relationships.

- One idea for developing a growth mindset, curiosity, and interest in learning is to use essential questions as a key part of the learning process. Review the criteria (page 24) for essential questions and write some essential questions that you might use to frame a specific learning experience.

- What are the most important skills we want students to practice and be able to perform well as part of a lifelong learning education? Based on your review and analysis of the skills suggested in this chapter, and on your own educational experiences, what would you suggest that teachers and schools do to better ensure that students develop these skills?

- Review the concept of deep learning and the examples provided in the deep learning section of this chapter (page 32). Based on this review, can you think of one or more good examples of deep learning that you experienced as a learner? Suggest several additional ways that teachers might deepen learning in schools and classrooms and provide specific examples.

- Review the chapter section on broadening and enriching student experiences (page 33). Based on this review, brainstorm a list of ways to improve and broaden student enrichment experiences and opportunities in both classrooms and schools.

Action Steps—Chapter 1

The following actions are suggested starting places for adopting and implementing lifelong learning goals.

- Use the four lifelong learning goals discussed in this chapter to design a lifelong learning mission or vision statement for a classroom, school, or district. Wording for such a statement could begin as "The mission (vision) of [teacher, classroom, school, district] is to . . . ." List several action steps that teachers and schools might take as a result of adopting this statement.

- Write a profile of the ideal graduating student from a lifelong learning perspective. What would the student understand if the lifelong learning goals described in this chapter were in place? What skills would this person have developed? What would be growth mindset indicators for a graduating student? Now, work backward from your ideal graduating student's profile and determine some examples of the action steps that teachers might adopt, at any level, to help students progress toward that profile.

- In the reproducible "Goals, Experiences, and Suggestions," identify your own educational experiences that are examples of the lifelong learning goals described in this chapter. For example, what types of experiences increased your growth mindset? Taught you how to develop understanding? Taught you how to do research? Then suggest some sample activities or strategies for as many goals as you can that might be used to put the goals into practice.

Goals, Experiences, and Suggestions

Identify some of your own educational experiences illustrating each goal in practice and suggest activities or strategies that you might use to put the goals into practice.

Goals	Educational Experiences	Improvement Suggestions
Develop a growth mindset.		
Build a foundation of content understanding (not a superficial knowledge base).		

page 1 of 2

Teaching for Lifelong Learning © 2021 Elliott Seif • SolutionTree.com
Visit **go.SolutionTree.com/21stcenturyskills** to download this free reproducible.

Build a foundation of skills. • Develop understanding. • Research and inquire. • Think at high levels. • Communicate effectively. • Collaborate. • Apply or transfer learning to new situations.		
Create independent learners who can dig deeply into learning.		
Broaden and enrich student experiences.		

Teaching for Lifelong Learning © 2021 Elliott Seif • SolutionTree.com
Visit **go.SolutionTree.com/21stcenturyskills** to download this free reproducible.

CHAPTER 2

Adapting Instruction for Lifelong Learning

I think a lot of traditional teachers think of themselves as the middle-men or -women between Newton and Darwin and the students—someone has discovered the knowledge, and their job is to get it into students' heads. Our most compelling teachers . . . were trying to help students to own the standards of their fields or disciplines and also inspire them to get interested in their subjects in the long run.

—Jal Mehta

In chapter 1 (page 17), I defined and described four critical education goals educators can strive for that prepare students for lifelong learning. In this chapter, I suggest and describe an instructional approach that will help put into practice and integrate the goals into instruction and help teachers implement a lifelong learning education program.

The four instructional phases, and their related activities, are described in this chapter.

1. **Set the stage** by initiating student engagement, promoting curiosity and interest, identifying relevant prior learning, and providing a context for new learning.

2. **Build a foundation** of knowledge, understandings, and skills.

3. **Deepen learning** by having students dig deeper into content and learning independently and interdependently.

4. **Provide closure** by having students finalize and communicate the results of their work and continuing to develop understanding and skills.

Many people can identify with teaching someone to play a musical instrument, and the process of learning to play one is a good illustration of the four phases of instruction in practice.

A Musical Example

Since I teach piano, I will use piano instruction as an example. Beginning students usually come to study piano with curiosity and an interest in learning how to play the piano (or at least the parents want them to learn). As the learning process begins, I *set the stage* by creating some initial experiences to build greater curiosity, pique interest, and determine prior knowledge. I talk with students about the types of music they like, why they want to learn to play the piano, and what they already know about playing the piano. I also introduce some basics, and we discuss the importance of regular practice and set up a schedule.

After this initial phase, I move to a second phase when I develop a *foundation of musical understanding and skills*. I introduce popular, easy-to-learn songs. I progressively challenge students to learn songs in many genres geared to their abilities and to learn the fundamentals of music and music theory. We host a few recitals for parents and others.

As students build a solid foundation, I move into a third phase that *deepens student learning*, allowing for *independent and interdependent activity*. I provide less guided practice and limit coaching. They begin to play and interpret more complex music on their own and perform formally at musical recitals. Music becomes more of a shared experience for students, who might play in a band or otherwise share their musical abilities with others.

Finally, there is a fourth phase during which students *refine and polish their work*, share their learning with others, and continue to grow and improve. My students often continue studying with me, with someone else, or independently, with occasional lessons to reinforce and refine what they are learning. They might give recitals. Sometimes they decide to learn another instrument. Sometimes the end result is simply strong knowledge and understanding of music in all its variety that become part of a lifelong musical experience.

Overview: The Four Phases of Instruction

This piano instruction example illustrates how to use a four-phase instructional planning and teaching model to design instruction for implementing lifelong learning goals. This four-phase model is not designed to plan individual lessons; rather, it is built around an arc of instruction: a cycle of learning as defined by a teacher. The traditional unit of study is one way of defining this arc, but the arc might also consist of the reading of a chapter book in an elementary classroom, or a yearlong senior-year high school capstone project culminating in project presentations. Each phase of this arc includes a set of activities designed to integrate the goals of lifelong learning identified in chapter 1 (page 17): developing a growth mindset, building a foundation of key understandings and skills, deepening learning, and broadening and enriching student experiences.

The instructional phases and associated activities are not designed as a formula or strict sequence, but rather as a set of flexible instructional planning tools that help teachers build lifelong learning goals into their instruction. Some teachers might see this instructional approach as a way to plan a sequence of learning activities that move from setting the stage, to foundational and then deep learning, and finally to closure, while others might engage students in activities that combine and integrate many aspects of all four phases at the same time. For example, during the foundation-building stage, students might do an independent or small-group activity that begins the process of deepening learning. Or, during the deepening-learning phase, the teacher might introduce students to a new research skill that builds on their skill development foundation.

Phase One: Setting the Stage

In a more traditional beginning to a unit of study, student curiosity and interest in learning are at best a secondary consideration and are often ignored. A teacher often introduces a unit by posting and sharing behavior objectives, and then conducts one or more brief introductory activities that may or may not pique student interest. Students often have limited involvement throughout these introductory activities.

Contrast this approach with the types of activities in the first phase of lifelong learning instruction. In this phase, a teacher initiates instruction so that students:

- Explore the meaningful goals, questions, and challenges that make up the new learning

- Understand the context for the new learning

- Examine any major tasks and activities that they will undertake

- Activate prior knowledge and skills to build on already-developed learning

Phase Two: Building the Foundation

During this phase, teachers encourage students to find out more about and develop a better understanding of the topic under study. They focus on developing a foundation of skills and demonstrating skills through guided practice. They share models and examples of student work and provide students with feedback to help them improve their understanding, skills, and work.

Major teaching goals during this phase are for students to do the following.

- Continue to build, sustain, and maintain a growth mindset and curiosity and interest in learning.

- Develop, practice, and grow a core foundation of understandings and skills.

Examples of foundational learning practices include the following.

- Actively researching, reading, evaluating, and processing information and ideas from multiple sources, including a textbook

- Learning how to take notes and develop connections and relationships through sequencing and concept formation

- Demonstrating knowledge and understanding by summarizing in one's own words and explaining key ideas

- Analyzing and interpreting information and data

- Creating persuasive arguments

- Writing, reflecting, and discussing in order to develop coherent thoughts, share ideas, and build listening and speaking skills

- Practicing complex and creative problem solving

- Working with others to build and grow foundational skills and learn collaboration skills

Phase Three: Deepening Learning

During the third phase, students deepen their learning and move toward more independent learning. At this point the student is developing *automaticity*, which, as pointed out in chapter 1, allows students to automatically, without paying full attention, apply a skill to a new learning situation (Bloom, 1986). Examples abound: The musician who quickly and easily can read and perform a piece of music; a chess master who quickly understands and can respond to an opponent's moves; a science researcher who can quickly initiate an experiment; and the plumber who quickly diagnoses and fixes a problem. In education, it is the student who can organize a research project on his or her own, create a compare-and-contrast diagram with limited help from the teacher, or write a persuasive essay with little teacher help or support.

Deeper learning also occurs when students have a chance to choose an interest and develop related skills and understandings. In their book *In Search of Deeper Learning: The Quest to Remake the American High School*, education scholars Mehta and Fine (2019) describe how their research demonstrates the importance of enrichment activities and programs for students, explaining that students enthusiastically state enrichment experiences:

> [The experiences] have the depth, authenticity, and creative ethos that their core disciplinary classes tend to lack. These extracurricular spaces are not only more fun and engaging, but also are actually more consistent with what we know makes for good platforms for learning. (p. 234)

Some enrichment activities work in classrooms, especially at the elementary level, where there are more flexible time periods. Checkers, chess, Scrabble, enriching video games—all can be incorporated into the classroom experience. Schools might offer such opportunities during advisory time or as extracurriculars at the middle and high school levels, or incorporate them into an enrichment club period during the day.

During the deepening learning phase of instruction, major teaching goals are for students to do the following.

- Deepen their understanding of key concepts and ideas that they already have learned.

- Independently apply their already-developed skills in order to explain their reasoning, build and test concepts and theories, create interpretations, conduct analyses, think creatively, and solve authentic problems.

- Learn independently or interdependently, often with limited support or guidance from a teacher.

- Choose an interest and develop and deepen their learning in this area of interest over time.

Phase Four: Providing Closure

Finally, there is a fourth phase, during which students refine and polish their work, share their learning with others, and continue growing and improving. The term *closure* is used here to reflect the reality that, for most classroom experiences, a unit comes to an end and a new learning experience begins. However, *closure* is not meant to imply that the learning of the same or similar understandings and foundational skills will not continue during a new unit of study.

While providing closure, major types of activities are as follows.

- Complete a product or products.

- Demonstrate and explain what they have learned, make presentations, and share their work with others.

- Continue learning, digging deeper into the topic and questions by learning from others and developing still greater understanding and better use of skills.

A Four-Phase Example

What can the four-phase instructional model look like when put into practice in classrooms? Here is an example from an English language arts unit, where elementary students are reading a book that has an interesting theme.

In phase one, the teacher introduces the book, provides some context for its narrative, introduces its theme to build interest and curiosity, asks students what they already know about the theme, and begins a discussion of a question that the students will explore together while they are reading the book.

In phase two, the teacher reads the book with students, introduces and defines new vocabulary words and concepts, asks questions about the text while reading aloud, and asks students to create a graphic organizer that visually illustrates the story's main narrative.

Once the second phase builds the foundation for the book, the teacher moves to phase three, asking the opening question that the class discussed in phase one—only this time the teacher asks if the book has helped answer the question. When students give their opinions, they must back them with evidence from the book. Everyone also discusses and expounds on their own ideas about the book's theme.

Finally, the teacher begins providing closure in phase four, asking students to write (or dictate) a brief reflection of the book—what they liked about it, what they learned as a result of reading and discussing it, and how they would *now* answer the question explored at the beginning of the unit. The teacher supports students as they rewrite to improve grammar, vocabulary, and meaning. Students share final reflections, and parents and guardians receive the writings for discussion with their children. Students may also go on to read other books on their own, either by the same author or that have the same theme.

Underlying Principles of Lifelong Learning Instruction

As you have read through the four-phase instructional planning and teaching model, and the examples so far described in this chapter, you may have noticed the following common principles underlying this approach.

1. Students learn best when they are active researchers.

2. Students learn best when they productively struggle and work independently.

3. Students learn best when they grow and improve through assessment and feedback.

4. Students learn best when they revisit and refine key learnings over time via learning progressions.

See the reproducible "Lifelong Learning Instruction Recommendations" (page 78) for a tool you can use to incorporate these principles into classroom and school activities.

Research–Based Learning

Research-based learning, a concept developed from my work with teachers over many years, is an essential feature of, and a way of thinking about, lifelong learning instruction. The term *research*, which often conjures up a picture of students writing research reports, is more loosely defined here. Instead of passively taking in information, students in research-based learning do the following.

*   Find interest and value in learning.

*   Define and explore problems and challenges.

*   Focus learning around core understandings and questions that guide inquiry and research.

*   Search through multiple sources for information and ideas.

*   Evaluate the sources for biases of information and ideas.

- Find patterns and synthesize information.
- Interpret materials.
- Develop arguments.
- Think critically and creatively.

Research-based learning builds an active and interactive approach into the instructional process that emphasizes the student's engagement and role in inquiry and learning. Learning becomes more student centered. In common language, teachers often begin their instruction with a question or challenge and the words "Let's find out more about this" or "Let's figure this out together," taking their students on a group learning quest (Fraser, 2018).

Productive Struggle and Independent Learning

According to education author Barbara R. Blackburn (2018), "Productive struggle is . . . the 'sweet spot' in between scaffolding and support." She warns that helping students when they initially run into challenges doesn't result in their working independently through them, and that "that may sound counterintuitive, . . . for students to become independent learners, they must learn to persist in the face of challenge" (Blackburn, 2018).

A good metaphor for learning as productive struggle is when a child learns to ride a bike. A parent does not do the riding for the child. What good would that do? The parent is the coach who is explaining, helping, and aiding. It is the child who is struggling, who does the work, who takes responsibility, and who finally completes the goal: independently riding without the parent's help!

Mathematics teacher David Ginsburg (2015) describes how he learned how to get his students to productively struggle with a class who had failed algebra and was repeating the course. Nothing seemed to work to turn this class around, until he shared interesting, common, and fun mathematics puzzles and problems with his students. His students began to work on these problems both individually and in small groups, got involved in the process, and repeatedly told him to let them figure out the answers without his help. Here's what he learned from this exercise: "Teachers often do more for students by doing less for students" (Ginsburg, 2015). In other words, letting his students productively struggle to find answers to these problems that interested them was a way to involve his students actively in learning mathematics and take greater responsibility for their own learning. It was the beginning of getting his students to productively struggle with algebra and thus take on the struggle to learn and grow.

In the lifelong learning instruction examples described in this chapter, students are continually struggling productively as they learn. Students try on new pieces of music, regularly practice to improve piano skills, and take responsibility for their own learning. In playing a sport, students productively struggle as they scrimmage, practice, and learn new strategies.

Giving students the chance to do the work, explain their thinking, solve problems, write in their own words, develop patterns, and make connections is what productive struggle is all about. We can't do it for them! This also means we need to give our students greater responsibility for the learning that they do. Threaded throughout the four phases of instruction and the suggested activities later in this chapter is the idea that students need to productively struggle and take greater responsibility for their own learning.

Growth and Improvement Through Assessment and Feedback

A key element across all phases of lifelong learning instruction is the opportunity to continually improve. Opportunities to develop a growth mindset—the belief that "your basic qualities are things you can cultivate through your efforts" through practice, hard work, and helpful feedback—are the key to improvement (Dweck, 2006, p. 7). Creating a growth mindset is a major part of learning and improving.

Unfortunately, in too many classrooms, especially at middle and high schools, there is often little opportunity for students to improve their work over time. The overabundance of knowledge to be learned and remembered, the fast pace of learning, the focus on transmission of knowledge, the final exam that ends learning—all of these typical classroom approaches make it difficult to find the time and inclination to assess for learning, provide feedback, and give opportunities for improvement. Based on their major study of high school learning, Mehta and Fine (2019) put it this way:

> Another pattern was mistaking faster for deeper. We saw this in classrooms across curricular levels . . . Teachers felt responsible for meeting external pacing expectations—whether they came from districts, state tests, SAT IIs, or APs—and the result was that they felt obligated to move through material quickly but not necessarily deeply. In science in particular, labs were often rushed efforts to demonstrate what the textbook said

> rather than opportunities for real investigation. In math or chemistry classes it became about learning more rules or molecules. Students who wanted to do well in school (or whose parents wanted them to) would comply with teachers' requests and do the expected homework and in-class tasks, but the goal was the grade and not [learning] the subject. (p. 27)

One key focus of the four phases of instruction is providing more time and opportunities for diagnosing students' previous learning, developing drafts of student work that they improve with time, providing peer and teacher feedback that enables students to improve their work, and sharing and celebrating final work. See more about ways to improve learning and promote a growth mindset in chapter 3 (page 81).

Learning Progressions

Teachers use the four phases of instruction to build a progression of student learning through initial assessment of previous learning, foundational development, and deeper and independent learning over time. Each lesson is meant to add to the student's knowledge, understanding, skills, and habits of mind. Sometimes teachers have setbacks and sometimes progress fails to materialize, but the goal is to continually help students progress toward greater knowledge, understanding, and skills, starting with beginner-level learning, then building a foundation, then moving toward advanced, deeper learning and experiences that foster greater independence and expertise.

In the same way, classroom instruction that supports growth and improvement goes through a progression of learning experiences that continually develop more complex understandings and skills (Kim & Care, 2018). Students build greater understanding and more complex skill development each time a teacher returns to and builds on previous learning of an understanding or skill. For example, in phase one, setting the stage, a third-grade teacher diagnoses what students already know and are able to do as readers, and then, in phase two, building the foundation, builds on previous reading strategies and vocabulary learned in the second grade to continue making progress in comprehension, conceptual understanding, and reading skills. A high school social studies teacher sets the stage for learning by diagnosing what students already know about eras in U.S. history, and then builds on previous understanding in order to create a more complex and nuanced understanding of the Constitution, the American Revolution, the Civil War, World War II, and so on. A middle school science teacher first discovers what students know and understand about the scientific method, and then continues building a foundation of skills related to science experimentation, question formulation, hypothesis testing, and results summarization.

When learning progressions are part of the instructional approach, teachers are all working toward the same goals for students: greater understanding of the world around them; increased ability to practice and use the skills identified for lifelong learning; and the development of a growth mindset that makes it likely students will continue to be interested in learning and want to continue doing so even after graduating. With a learning progression mindset, no one teacher has a monopoly on growth, improvement, and depth. Each teacher is part of a larger system moving students toward greater expertise and independence as learners.

Phase-Related Instructional Strategies

Specific types of instructional strategies implement each of the four phases. For example, setting-the-stage strategies focus on ways to diagnose previous student learning, raise interest and curiosity, and provide a context for new learning. Building-a-foundation strategies provide ways for students to develop conceptual understanding and practice their skills with help and support. Deepening-learning strategies promote independent and interdependent learning and also support students so they can dig deeper into the content and apply learned skills to new areas of learning. Closure strategies provide students with the opportunity to complete and evaluate their work, share their results with others, and continue to learn and grow.

Examples of classroom strategies for each of the four phases are provided in the following sections. Note that many other strategies are also described in multiple resources that can aid teachers in discovering a variety of ways to put the four-phase instructional model into practice (Himmele & Himmele, 2017; Hyerle, 2009; McTighe & Silver, 2020).

Phase One Strategies

When planning strategies that align with the setting-the-stage phase, teachers should devise activities that motivate students, help them understand the challenges, goals, and major tasks of a unit of study, and explore the context for the unit. Additionally, such activities enable a teacher to learn more about the knowledge and skills that students bring to the topic under study. The following setting-the-stage activities are just a few of many possibilities that initiate student engagement and tap into their interest and curiosity.

- Activators

- Goal sharing and question discussions

- Productive question development

- Context providers
- KWL activity
- Arts and artifact activities

Activators

Activators are designed to help the teacher discover and diagnose students' prior knowledge and skills related to the unit's goals, create and pique student interest in the topic, and establish a context for learning (Saphier & Haley, 1993a; Schrock, n.d.). Some activator examples follow, and all are adaptable to all grade levels.

- Ask students to brainstorm their ideas about a topic under study. For example, ask students to brainstorm their responses to the question, What environmental problems exist? As students share their questions, determine what they already know about the topic and select questions to examine for future learning.

- Engage the class in a write 3-2-1 exercise. For example, ask students to list three things they already know about a topic, two things they'd like to know about or learn more about, and one question they have about the topic (Saphier & Haley, 1993b; Wormeli, 2005).

- Ask students to draw a picture or diagram representing what they already know about this topic and share their responses with the class.

- Begin a student journal for a unit by having students complete prompts, such as, *I'm excited about studying this unit because . . . , I think this topic will be interesting because . . .* , and *While studying this topic, I would really like to learn about . . . .*

- Read a compelling story, paragraph, or quote to introduce a theme or idea. Use the story, paragraph, or quote to ask students to raise questions about the theme or idea.

- Introduce a mystery, puzzle, or problem that stimulates interest in studying the unit. For example, mathematics puzzles and problems are good for stimulating interest in a mathematics unit.

Goal Sharing and Question Discussions

Teachers use goal sharing and question discussions to initially introduce students to key understandings, essential questions, and challenges that form the basic goals of the unit of study and promote interest and curiosity. For example, in studying the American Revolution, teachers might share with students that a goal is to understand that the war was a rebellion against British rule. After sharing the unit's major goal, a teacher might introduce the following essential question: What do you think causes people to rebel against those in power? and then hold an initial discussion to determine how students at the beginning of the unit might answer the question or develop additional questions for the unit.

Productive Question Development

Productive question development introduces students to the unit theme or topic and then asks them to create the questions to explore (Fraser, 2018). One way to accomplish this is for students, in small groups or as a large group, to brainstorm questions that are of interest to them around a theme or topic under study, and then to have them sort and combine them into larger questions and ideas. The students and the teacher then decide which groups of questions they will explore and answer as the unit of study progresses (Lee, 2019).

Another way to create productive questions is for teachers and students to use the Question Formulation Technique, developed through the Right Question Institute (n.d.). This technique calls for students to follow these four steps.

1. Generate a set of questions based on the topic using the following rules.
   ◇ Ask as many questions as you can.
   ◇ Do not stop to discuss, judge, or answer any question.
   ◇ Write down every question exactly as it is stated.
   ◇ Change statements into questions.
2. Brainstorm as many questions as possible.
3. Improve the questions by determining which are closed ended (have one right answer) and which are open ended (have many possible answers). See if you can make closed-ended questions open ended.
4. Select three open-ended questions that the class considers the most important, or those that you must address first, or those you want to explore further.

Context Providers

Context providers enable students to develop the background knowledge that helps them understand time, place, and key background ideas, concepts, and events. Any of the following can provide useful context, depending on the content area, subject, and grade level.

- Brief introductory readings that include background knowledge and understanding

- Media presentations on topics such as historical eras, science explanations, artist backgrounds, mathematics discoverers, and book contexts

- Songs and stories that illustrate stories and music set during historical events

- Biographies about people who lived during historical periods, literary figures, famous scientists and mathematicians, artists, and inventors

- Problems, dilemmas, and challenges that occurred in a historical period, led to a scientific discovery or an invention, or led to the writing of a piece of fiction

KWL Activity

The KWL activity uses a three-column chart designed to introduce a unit of study. It works with any subject and at any grade level, although it is probably best used from upper elementary through high school. KWL helps a teacher discover *what students already know* about a unit (K), what they *wonder* about and *want* to learn more about (W), and what they are *learning* as they progress through the unit (L; National Education Association, n.d.; Ogle, 1986). A variation, KWHL, uses a four-column chart to also ask students *how they can learn more* about the topic (H).

Arts and Artifact Activities

Arts and artifact activities introduce students to a work of art, a photo, or an artifact that creates a mystery for interest building and discussion. For example, a teacher might show photos of people living in Ethiopia or artifacts of Nigerian life to introduce a unit about African cultures, having students describe what they see and what the items suggest about the lives of people, or to hypothesize about where the artifacts are from, why the artifacts were created, what they represent, or how they might be interpreted.

Phase Two Strategies

The strategies in this section help build a student's foundation of understandings and skills. While there are many types of strategies useful for building a foundation, the following strategies can help students develop key concepts, make connections, develop relationships, understand what they read, improve writing skills, develop research skills, and strengthen cooperative learning skills:

- Guided concept-development activities
- Sequencing and patterning activities
- Reading-for-understanding activities
- Writing process and writer's workshop
- Research-inquiry skill-building activities
- Thinking routine activities
- Cooperative learning activities

Guided Concept-Development Activities

Guided concept-development activities help students "identify big ideas and conceptual understandings" (McTighe & Silver, 2020). Students learn how to develop concepts from multiple sets of facts and data. They are able to construct their understanding of important concepts by learning how to sort, group, categorize, classify, label, define, connect, and apply newly developed concepts to new situations and circumstances.

Classification is one type of guided concept-development activity (Marzano, 2019). In classification activities, students get a set of items related to a topic, such as animals, plants, words illustrating the lifestyles of British colonists, and so on. Students are asked to group these words in ways that make sense to them, and to label the groups and define their characteristics. In a class discussion, students identify their groups and labels and explain their thinking. The teacher might then suggest a grouping that reflects the thinking of scientists or historians to illustrate another way of conceptualizing key terms.

Concept attainment is another guided concept-development activity (McTighe & Silver, 2020; Silver, Strong, & Perini, 2007). The teacher chooses a concept to develop (revolution, scientific investigation, variable, and so on). Students are then provided with both positive and negative examples of the concept, one example at a time (this is a *yes* example of the concept, this is a *no* example). Once they have seen at least three yes and no examples, students suggest their own examples and then define the concept.

Sequencing and Patterning Activities

Sequencing and patterning activities enable students to create causal chains of events, narratives, and patterns that provide the basis for developing and understanding basic causal links, mathematical patterns, and so on. For example, timelines give students the opportunity to create a sequence of events and experiences that also might illustrate a causal chain. Many types of visual tools, including graphic organizers, let students form different types of patterns and sequences (Hyerle, 2009). Google has a site (https://bit.ly/3b6nM9M) with different types, and you can search online for literature graphic organizers and find many, including Laura Candler's Teaching Resources (https://bit.ly/3rQ5LT6); others exist that help students develop information webs and brainstorm associations (Hyerle, 2009).

More examples follow.

- **Character web:** Describe how a character in literature or person in history might act or feel, what they might say, or how they might look.

- **Cause-and-effect chart:** Document a single cause with multiple effects.

- **Concept wheel:** Describe the parts of a concept.

- **Flow map:** Illustrate or plan sequencing, steps, and stages.

- **Important contributions chart:** Map a person's contributions.

- **Persuasion map:** Link information to support a thesis, goal, or hypothesis.

- **Question frame:** Develop higher-level questions about a topic.

- **Venn diagram:** Display similarities and differences between two items.

Reading-for-Understanding Activities

These activities help students learn how to go below the surface and find the deeper meaning in what they are reading. Literacy educator Kelly Gallagher (2004) describes reading for understanding this way:

> We can assign reading in our classrooms, give students shallow reading assignments, and have students pass them. On the surface, everything looks fine: the students read the text and are able to answer the questions. But in reality, do they really understand what they have read? They can answer surface level questions, but once you ask them to evaluate, to analyze, to synthesize, they can't do it. (pp. 4–5)

One of the most comprehensive approaches for improving reading across all content areas is the before-during-after reading strategy approach. Psychiatrist Sue Beers and educator Lou Howell (2003) have collected and created multiple reading strategies for teachers to use before, during, and after reading that promote understanding.

Before-reading strategy examples follow.

- **Categories! Categories! Categories!:** Students classify reading and background knowledge items, such as vocabulary terms, into categories. They then discuss their categories and explain why they created them.

- **Feature Story:** The teacher introduces and discusses the key text features— for example, the key parts of a book, headings in each part, items which are in italics or bold lettering, and key charts and graphs—before students begin reading.

- **Front-Load the Words:** Teachers and students address key new vocabulary prior to reading by identifying and defining the most important words to know for a reading assignment.

During-reading strategy examples follow.

- **Agree or Disagree:** Teachers present students with an agree-disagree statement related to a reading. As they read, students use information and ideas gleaned from the reading to agree or disagree with the statement, and cite evidence from the text to support their position.

- **Another Kind of Outline:** Students use a two-column organizer to create an outline for a reading. As they read, students list big ideas or key concepts in the left column and supporting or explanatory details about the big ideas or key concepts in the right column. A class discussion afterward lets them share their big ideas, concepts, and details and come to a common understanding.

- **Chain Reaction:** As students read, they develop a sequence of significant events or steps in a process, with details about the events noted as part of the sequence. Students can then share their sequence of events in a gallery walk, where other students can comment on whether the events are in proper order and what the meaning of the sequence is to the larger story.

After-reading strategy examples follow.

- **Bar Graph:** Students create a bar graph based on data in a reading, use the bar graph to summarize data and conclusions, and generate follow-up questions.

- **One Word to Sum It All Up:** Students sum up their learning with a single word and support their word choice with evidence from the reading. They discuss their responses and compare and contrast the words chosen.

- **What If?:** Students summarize what happened in a story and then create a different ending or outcome. They then write what would happen in the story if this ending or outcome occurred. Students share and discuss their ideas in order to imagine different endings and results.

Other examples of reading-for-understanding activities appear in works by Emelina Minero (2018) and Ruth Schoenbach, Cynthia Greenleaf, Christine Cziko, and Lori Hurwitz (1999).

Writing Process and Writer's Workshop

The writing process and writer's workshop are two ways to build a foundation of writing skills that also enhance the development of many other skills (Calkins & Mermelstein, 2003; Lenter, 2012; Peha, 2003). The writing process consists of five stages of writing: (1) prewriting activities that narrow down a topic, determine the purpose of writing, and create an outline of ideas and information, (2) initial writing that results in a draft (putting down points and ideas on paper and organizing the ideas for writing), (3) revising to improve the work (refining ideas, rethinking how text is organized, and rewriting to improve meaning), (4) editing elements such as grammar, mechanics, and spelling, and (5) publishing (submitting the final work to a source, such as a teacher or community experts).

The process encourages students to ask good questions and formulate writing ideas in the prewriting stage, process and organize information in the initial writing phase, reflect on their writing and get quality feedback, rewrite, edit for clarity, and share their writing with others.

The writer's workshop devotes specific class time solely to writing, and students are treated as budding authors. Literacy consultant Steve Peha (2003) notes:

> As in professional writing workshops, emphasis is placed on sharing work with the class, on peer conferencing and editing, and on the collection of a wide variety of work in a

writing folder, and eventually in a portfolio. Teachers write with their students and share their own work as well. The workshop setting encourages students to think of them-selves as writers, and to take their writing seriously. (p. 3)

Research-Inquiry Skill-Building Activities

Research-inquiry skill-building activities enable students to select multiple reliable, valid sources of information to begin to answer questions and better understand main ideas and concepts. Teachers can use these activities to teach basic research skills, helping students learn how to find relevant and reliable resources related to the topic under study, to read and develop key vocabulary and concepts, and to analyze and synthesize information and data from various types of materials (Fraser, 2018).

- **Note taking and other guided study-skill activities:** These provide students with ways to collect, evaluate, sort, organize, and synthesize readings and other sources of information. Several note-taking methods follow (California Polytechnic State University, n.d.).

    ◇ *Outlining:* Students record a lecture's or text's main point and then add subpoints. Information is outlined from a big main idea to smaller, specific details.

    ◇ *Cornell notetaking:* A page is organized into three sections. The upper part of the page is divided into two columns, the left column smaller than the one on the right. The right column is used for jotting notes from a book, lecture, or media presentation and includes main points, facts, ideas, and so on. The left column is for writing questions, big ideas, or helpful ways to remember what is in the right column. After these two columns are complete, the bottom third of the page is for writing a brief summary of what was learned.

    ◇ *Mind mapping:* Students create a visual outline—a web— of their ideas that they have learned related to a topic.

These methods can be taught to students to help them organize, remember, and understand what they have read and heard.

- **Representation of data activities:** These provide students the opportunity to learn how to represent and display quantitative data. Students examine and learn how to develop charts, tables, and other graphical approaches in order to summarize, organize, and display data.

- **Summarizers:** Students demonstrate what they have learned and understand at the end of a learning period. Summarizer activities help students to integrate and synthesize new ideas with previous learning, figure out what learning is important, and summarize and reflect on what they have learned (Saphier & Haley, 1993b; Wormeli, 2005). Teachers can use summarizer activities to ascertain how well students understand the content being studied and adjust their lessons to ensure that students have developed the foundational knowledge expected of them. The following are examples of summarizer activities.

  ◇ *ABC:* Students summarize content using the letters of the alphabet as starting points. For example, high school students might use the ABC method to summarize what they have learned about the Renaissance. One student might list the following items: *art, Bondone, city-state, Dante.* Instead of writing words, prewriters might draw pictures to summarize their learning.

  ◇ *Learning log:* Students free write about what they have learned. This works for any subject or topic.

  ◇ *A picture-diagram:* Students summarize their learning by drawing a picture or creating a diagram at the end of an instructional period.

  ◇ *3-2-1 writing exercise:* Students write three main ideas learned, two key facts learned, and one question they still have about what they learned. The teacher collects the writings to identify what main points students learned and what to explore in the following lesson (Saphier & Haley, 1993b; Wormeli, 2005).

Thinking Routine Activities

Thinking routines are strategies that a teacher can use at any grade level. The routines enable students to develop specific thinking habits and strategies around three major types of thinking: introducing and exploring ideas; synthesizing and organizing ideas; and digging deeper into ideas (Ritchhart, Church, & Morrison, 2011). For example, Ron Ritchhart and colleagues (2011) describe how the routine question *What makes you say that?*, when used as a regular part of the classroom discourse, helps students dig deeper into ideas, and specifically helps students learn how to give reasons with evidence. Table 2.1 lists three examples of the thinking routines, one for each of the three thinking routine categories. Many additional resources are available for helping teachers learn how to teach so as to improve thinking (Barell, 2006; Stobaugh, 2019; Wasserman, 2009).

TABLE 2.1: Thinking Routines

Routine	What It Looks Like	What It Promotes
Think-puzzle-explore	Ask students what they think they know about a topic. Then ask them what puzzles them about the topic. Finally, ask them how we might investigate and explore this topic.	*Introducing and exploring ideas:* Connecting to prior knowledge, raising the level of curiosity and interest, deciding on how to go about investigating and exploring
Connect-extend-challenge	Ask students how new learning connects to what they already know. Ask students to consider how new learning extends their learning, taking it in new or deeper directions. Finally, ask what puzzles or challenges this new learning has raised for you.	*Synthesizing and organizing ideas:* Synthesizing new ideas with previous knowledge; identifying how their ideas and knowledge have broadened, deepened, or expanded
Claim-support-question	First identify a claim of fact or belief about a topic, issue, or idea being studied. Then ask what supports the claim. Then raise questions about the credibility of the claim, and share student responses.	*Digging deeper into ideas:* Probing "truth" claims, looking for support, looking for problems with credibility

Source: Adapted from Ritchhart et al., 2011.

Cooperative Learning Activities

Studies over many years demonstrate that cooperative learning activities positively affect student achievement, especially when cooperative groups have clear goals and individual accountability is built into the assessment process (Roseth, Johnson, & Johnson, 2008; Slavin, 2014). Many different types of strategies support the practice and development of cooperative learning skills. Some of these follow.

- **Jigsaws:** Jigsaws enable students to collaborate with and learn from each other. To prepare a jigsaw activity, the teacher puts students into groups and gives them an assignment that can only be completed if each member of the group provides his or her piece of the assignment. For example, students might each receive a sentence strip that lists one of the steps in the water cycle. The group's task would be to put all the strips in order. Jigsaw activities also often help students break down a major reading into different sections, each read by one person in a group. After students in their original groups have each read their assigned section, they convene with students from different groups who have been assigned the same passage; they discuss and summarize the main points of their reading. Everyone returns to their original groups to share and summarize the important points of each part of the reading, so that all class members learn the key ideas and information from the entire reading.

- **Fishbowls:** Conduct this activity periodically to organize discussions with a smaller number of students and to help improve the quality of discussions. Teachers ask a small group—between five to ten students—to get into the middle of the classroom and form a circle. Another group of students forms a second circle outside the first circle, with the rest of the class observing. The first circle gets a discussion question, often based on a current topic or something the class is reading, and discusses that question for five to ten minutes. Then the outer circle of students comments on the quality of the discussion using the following criteria: how many students participated, how well people listened to each other and asked clarifying questions, how well the group stayed on topic, and how well people used data and evidence to support their views. Once they finish commenting, a new group of five to ten students forms a discussion circle, with another group forming an outer circle. A second discussion commences for five to ten minutes. Then the new outer circle evaluates the discussion. This continues for as long as the teacher wants students to discuss the topic and evaluate the quality of discussion.

- **Problem-solving small groups:** Students are given a challenging task to complete in a small group, such as an open-ended assignment (page 91). Each member of the small group is assigned a role to play in the group to facilitate cooperation. Roles might include task leader, who begins the discussion and makes sure that the discussion stays on task; recorder, who takes notes on key points made by members of the group; questioner, who generates questions and involves all students; timekeeper; and encourager, who encourages all members of the group to participate. After the groups complete the challenging task, they share their results and discuss how well the group worked together and what problems they faced.

Phase Three Strategies

In phase three, students work independently or interdependently, with limited help and guidance, to deepen their learning and use the understandings and skills they learned in phase two and in other learning situations in new and novel ways. Here are some brief examples of the types of activities and strategies that might occur during this phase. In phase three, students work independently or collaboratively to accomplish the following.

- Complete a complex research project or performance task to evaluate and synthesize knowledge, understandings, and ideas from multiple sources.

- Conduct independent research on a topic chosen by the teacher or student.

- Develop a student-led discussion, with an open-ended question, on a topic examined in phase two.

- Compare and contrast multiple ideas learned in phase two.

- Develop science hypotheses and test them by designing and conducting experiments.

- Complete a complex research paper.

- Construct creative alternatives and solutions to challenging authentic problems.

- Develop and create a well-reasoned, logical, cogent argument for a position.

- Explain the process for arriving at a solution to a complex mathematics problem.

- Develop a complex interpretation of a reading, media presentation, artwork, or musical piece.

- Analyze historical documents or statistical data.

- Critique and analyze bias in sources of information, such as a textbook, TV reporting, social media, and news articles.

- Write an essay with a unique perspective and voice.

- Design and work on completing an authentic task that applies learning in complex ways.

- Use a rubric to judge their work alone or with peers and improve it.

Phase Four Strategies

In phase four, students complete and share the results and products they have developed during earlier phases of instruction. These might include products and activities such as the following.

- Reflective and analytical essays

- Position or research papers, persuasive essays, and other writing assignments

- Presentations and explanations of final products in authentic settings, such as to an audience of local politicians or experts in a field related to the work done, such as engineers, artists, or businesspeople

- Self-reflections (page 93)

- Multimedia products, such as podcasts and films

- Action plans that put the ideas and solutions developed by students into practice

Strategies for All Phases of Instruction

While in the previous section I briefly described activities that are useful during each of the four phases, in this section I describe activities that are useful during all four phases of instruction.

- Interactive notebooks

- Open-ended assignments

- Performance tasks and projects

- Visual learning tools

- Self-reflection activities

Educators can use and adapt each of these activities for all grade levels and cut across most or all of the four phases. In chapter 3 (page 81), I will also describe how the instructional activities in this section can work as major assessments for life-long learning.

Interactive Notebooks

Interactive notebooks provide a way for students to actively interact with what they are learning by collecting, organizing, synthesizing, and applying understandings and skills in meaningful ways. On the one hand, the notebooks enable students to record, collect, and organize information from a teacher, text, or additional resources. On the other hand, students complete more challenging assignments that help them see connections, perform analyses, synthesize data in interesting ways, and become independent, creative thinkers and writers.

Practically, many teachers have students organize their interactive notebooks by using one side of the notebook pages (left or right side) for recording and collecting information in traditional ways, and the other side of the page for processing information and ideas and thinking outside the box. Another way that teachers organize the notebook is to keep one section for notetaking, and another section where students create visual organizers, build theories, and creatively solve challenging problems. Figure 2.1 illustrates the features of interactive notebook pages.

Note-taking page: Class notes, reading summaries, and notes from other sources

Processing page: Concept development, interpretations, reactions, reflections, creative responses, and summaries

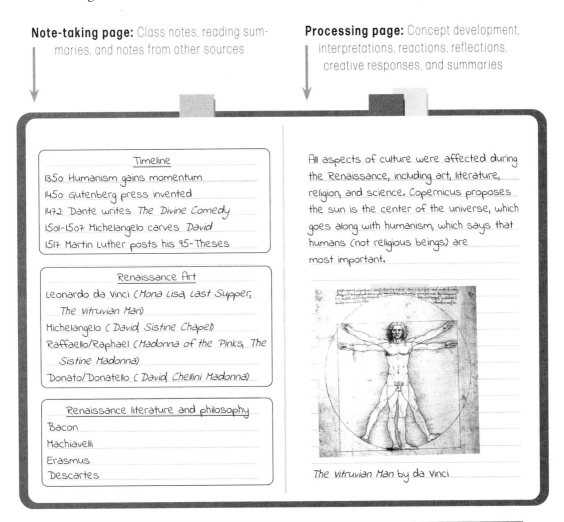

Figure 2.1: Interactive notebook pages example.

A sample of how to use interactive notebooks as a major learning resource, using science as an example, is featured in the book *Teaching Science With Interactive Notebooks* (Marcarelli, 2010).

Open-Ended Assignments

Open-ended assignments provide students with opportunities to complete writing tasks and participate in discussions with multiple possible responses. These challenging assignments propose questions and offer activities that lead students to think and explain rather than give simple *yes* or *no* answers (Bratslavsky, Wright, Kritselis, & Luftig, 2019; Gardner, 2005). They can provoke interest and curiosity in what is to be learned, teach understanding and foundational skills, and provide opportunities for independent and deeper learning.

The following verbs can spur ideas for open-ended assignments.

- *Organize, sort, categorize, classify*
- *Compare, contrast*
- *Judge, rank, prioritize, select*
- *Summarize, explain in your own words*
- *Create*
- *Predict*
- *Decide, choose*

Here are some sample open-ended assignments.

- When we take our trip to the local supermarket, choose three products that you think are healthy to eat. Explain why you picked them.
- Of all the people in history we studied this year, who was the greatest (most important, most ambitious, most creative, most outstanding)? Why do you think so?
- How would you organize and show the connections between all the information we have collected on adaptation?
- Do all organisms need the same things to live and grow? Choose two organisms and decide what they both might need to live and grow. Explain what's the same and what's different.
- We have studied country *X*. Explain what you think it might be like to live in a small town in this country, and then a large city in the country. Use the information we have gathered about this country to support your ideas.

- Was the character *X* in this book a good person? Why or why not? Support your view with evidence from the reading.

- How would you change the Constitution to update and improve it if you were given the opportunity? Give reasons for your answers.

You can create open-ended assignments by adapting more traditional assignments and tasks. For example, imagine asking students to solve the following mathematical problem.

Divide seven cookies equally among four partygoers.

The teacher can use the problem to make sure students are able to use the division algorithm and divide the seven cookies equally among four people: 7 divided by 4 = $\frac{7}{4} = 1\frac{3}{4}$. This approach leaves one right answer.

However, imagine changing the way you define the problem, as follows.

Divide seven cookies equally among four partygoers. Think of many different ways to solve this problem. Explain your answer. Show your work.

With this change, the assignment becomes open ended. Students are given the opportunity to be creative, define and solve the problem in a way that makes sense to them, and come up with many different ways of thinking about the problem and many different answers. Students might also work in small groups to solve this problem and come up with many different solutions. When the problem is opened up in this way, it can lead to all kinds of processes and answers. One unusual, original student response was to grind up the cookies and weigh out equal amounts so that all partygoers get the same weighed amount!

An additional way of incorporating open-ended assignments into the classroom is through Socratic seminars, sometimes called *interpretive discussions*. The seminars begin with open-ended questions designed to provoke discussion and to create meaning from a variety of types of texts, such as books, media, and news sources. They enable students to dig deeper into a specific text, examine its meaning, and use the text details to create, share, and discuss opinions, arguments, and perspectives (Copeland, 2005; Haroutunian-Gordon, 2014).

Socratic seminars may occur during any of the four phases of instruction. After introducing the open-ended assignment and initiating a discussion in phase one, a teacher might share discussion rules in phase two and model, practice, and lead good discussions based on the open-ended assignment. In phase three, students themselves might lead a discussion, and in phase four the teacher might have students reflect on the discussion process and its conclusions and continue discussing and revising the results.

Performance Tasks and Projects

Performance tasks and projects are investigative activities, conducted over time, in which students pursue answers to interesting, relevant questions and problems. They enable students to conduct meaningful research, develop answers to questions, and share solutions to problems. Students also complete and share a product or a performance, such as a research paper, poster, brochure, diorama, design, or artwork, and often present to other students or to an outside group of community members. Some performance tasks and projects present students with an authentic, real-life problem to solve, asking them to develop and share complex but realistic solutions that they then share with outside experts in the field, who evaluate their performance.

Performance tasks and projects often provide evidence of student understanding and demonstrate students' ability to apply their learning to new and novel situations. They are also ideal vehicles for applying and integrating academic content with life-long learning skills including research, critical thinking, creativity, collaboration, and communication (McTighe, Doubet, & Carbaugh, 2020).

Performance tasks and projects are usually introduced during the setting-the-stage phase of instruction and follow steps similar to these.

1. The teacher shares the goals, what students will do to complete the task or project, and some introductory activities, such as brainstorming useful resources, sharing presentation expectations, and so on.

2. Students conduct research, analyze information and data, and begin developing products or performances.

3. Students complete a draft of their work.

4. Teachers share feedback on the drafts, which students use to improve their work.

5. Students work independently to improve and complete the products or performances.

6. Students polish their work, share it with others, and continue their investigation with renewed interest and understanding.

The following are examples of different types of performance tasks and projects that support the development of a variety of lifelong learning goals.

- **Research projects:** Students develop all or part of a research project around a topic related to the curriculum or a topic of interest. For example, elementary students might search the internet for information related to a question of interest to them and select the most reliable sources of information. Information-processing activities—finding, noting, sorting, and synthesizing information and data—can be integrated into any unit in which students have a key question or theme to examine and find information (Fraser, 2018).

- **Reading for understanding projects:** At every level, students should be encouraged to read a wide variety of literature and texts, develop an understanding of the core ideas from that reading, and create interpretations and critiques of what they have read. Teachers may also ask students to reflect on both required and chosen literature by creating summaries, comments, and analyses. As students progress through the grades, they might also develop longer interpretive essays for their readings and learn how to write a coherent analysis for a piece of literature.

- **Scientific investigation projects:** At every level, students need to practice scientific investigation skills and apply the rules of science. Kindergarten students can investigate how plants survive; high school students can study how genetics affect organism survival. Beginning with preschool and through the high school years, students can make scientific observations, conduct experiments, and apply their learning by creating original experiments and investigations.

- **Persuasive writing projects:** At every grade level, students need to learn about and discuss past and current issues, examine many points of view and perspectives, and develop persuasive arguments. For example, consider the following task, which is designed for learning how to connect historical and scientific information with current events and issues: Students research a current issue or problem and its historical context, and then write a position paper that argues for a way to improve the situation or deal with the problem. They must also incorporate historical facts and understandings to illustrate a deeper understanding of the problem or issue. Examples of possible issues or problems include civil rights, pollution, poverty, inequality, climate change, medical research, and health care. The task also develops students' ability to write a coherent persuasive essay and gives students the opportunity to connect their learning to community experiences. In middle and high school, teachers may also ask students to find organizations and agencies that deal with the problem, interview people associated with these organizations, and volunteer with one or more of the organizations associated with the chosen problem and reflect on the volunteer work.

- **Health and physical well-being projects:** Schools usually provide students with a myriad of information about health and disease and use physical education classes to help students learn to play sports and games and to exercise. Although it is becoming more common, students have rarely been asked to answer such questions as, "How do I maintain my own health and physical well-being? What is a nutritionally appropriate diet? How do I maintain a vigorous lifestyle and physical fitness?" One appropriate project in this area is for students to learn how to combine health and physical information into a plan for healthful living and physical fitness. The healthful living design project might ask students to create a week-long model of a healthful menu tailored to their needs and tastes for a week, followed by a discussion of why it is healthful. The project could also ask students to develop a weekly exercise plan that they could realistically follow. Teachers can also include other aspects of healthful living, such as disease prevention.

- **Mathematical problem-solving projects:** Students may struggle to see a direct application or connection of mathematics to other subjects and to the outside world. One way students can learn mathematics principles and understand their applicability to the outside world and its connections to other subjects is to design a building, a city, or a playground. Such problem solving also helps students develop a variety of complex lifelong learning skills, such as critical and creative thinking. For example, researching and designing a dream house, including floor plans, a description of the interior, and materials to be used is an interdisciplinary mathematics project that has students working together in teams. Students also create a model of their homes and make a cost analysis for the interior of at least one room in the house. Finally, students would summarize the results of their work in a presentation (ENC Focus, 2002).

- **Art and career and technical education projects:** Students can develop and apply their knowledge and skills of one or more arts or career and technical education areas through the following choice of performance tasks and projects.

  ◇ Participate in a musical, dance, or theater performance.
  ◇ Write a piece of original music or theater.
  ◇ Create an original artwork.
  ◇ Describe a piece of artwork or music, place it in its historical context, and interpret its meaning.

  ◇ Develop a new recipe.

  ◇ Design a more efficient engine.

  ◇ Redesign a hotel room for greater comfort and
     better aesthetics.

• **Authentic projects:** Authentic projects enable students to solve complex,
  messy, real-life problems that have no obvious and easy solution. Learning
  tasks might be focused around issues such as improving ways to clean
  streets, addressing poverty, designing an ideal city, figuring out better ways
  to distribute food in a pandemic, designing a new game to help students
  learn mathematics, increasing the general population's health and wellness,
  or helping two countries solve long-term hostilities. Problem solving
  requires what Robert J. Sternberg (2019), professor of human development,
  calls an *adaptive intelligence* that enables students to redefine problems,
  review, research, and organize relevant information, develop and evaluate
  alternatives, suggest solutions, and develop implementation plans.

Here is one example of an authentic student task: Ninth-grade students in
an interdisciplinary mathematics and science course spent the school year
focusing on three essential questions: (1) How do things move?, (2) What
makes them move?, and (3) How can we describe that motion? The teacher
built the exploration of these questions around an authentic task: designing
an amusement park ride. First, the teacher introduced students to the
authentic learning task. She included many activities designed to provide
background knowledge and understanding of the key mathematics and
science concepts necessary to complete the task, such as inertia, centrifugal
force, and centripetal force. Students spent a day at a nearby amusement
park gathering data. Equipped with stop watches and a meter to measure
gravity, they analyzed the rides in the park. During the debriefing after the
trip, students discussed how the concepts they had learned applied to the
amusement park rides. During classes following the field trip, the teacher
pushed students to think about and deepen their knowledge to develop
their own original plans for an amusement park ride. Through the use of
challenging problems, she helped students examine the principles of time,
distance, velocity, acceleration, deceleration, and the relationships among
them, and discussed how these concepts relate to developing an amusement
park ride. During the final stage of the unit, students wrote an extensive
paper detailing their ride design, including diagrams, and providing
technical information to show that their design was realistic and doable.

- **Passion projects:** Passion projects are student-designed projects built around a student interest. For example, they can be developed around an author of interest, a career interest, a topic in a subject area, a musical or art interest, or a hobby. Passion projects can be part of the classroom or school experience at any level, or function as a culminating graduation project to ensure that students have developed lifelong learning skills. You can read more about these projects in *The Passion Project: A Teacher's Guide for Implementing Passion Projects in Your Classroom* (Lester, 2016).

Visual Learning Tools

Visual learning tools (also called *graphic organizers*) transform content:

> into active knowledge using a rich integration of modalities—visual, spatial, verbal, and numerical—to create conceptual rich models of their meaning. These acts of transformation take students from the basic information found in texts to the highest orders of thinking seamlessly, from building concrete content facts and vocabulary directly to the abstract conceptual understandings that are the basis for learning knowledge in every discipline (Hyerle, 2009, p. 2).

Another definition states that visual learning tools "help students collect information, make interpretations, solve problems, devise plans, and become aware of how they think" (Green, 2000, p. 1). Considerable research supports the value of using visual learning tools (Dean, Hubbell, Pitler, & Stone, 2012). "These strategies are powerful because they tap into students' natural tendency for visual image processing" (Dean et al., 2012, p. 64).

Visual learning tools can help a teacher in all four phases of instruction. For example, students can create or complete a visual organizer of their prior learning; they can help students visually organize new learning, synthesize and summarize learning, and produce a visual end product, such as a poster, to share with others. Multiple types of visual tools exist, including mind maps, picture webs, decision trees, analysis charts, before-and-after reading charts, story maps, and many more (McKnight, 2010, 2013).

Self-Reflection Activities

Self-reflection activities enable students to pull together their thoughts and experiences, and articulate, demonstrate, and reflect on their learning through journals, structured activities, and reflective essays. They are useful during all four phases of instruction. For example, in the setting-the-stage phase, self-reflections can help students recall what they have learned previously and think about how it relates to what they will be learning. Students can write what they know about the context of what they are about to learn. During phase two, self-reflections can help students summarize and explain their understandings and develop knowledge connections and relationships. During phase three, students can independently develop reflections on what they are learning, dig deeper into their learning, and apply their learning to new and novel situations. Finally, during closure in phase four, students can develop and present summaries and analyses of their learning to others.

Examples of the types of self-reflection activities that teachers might assign at any time during the K–12 experience and in any of the phases of instruction follow.

- **What I learned:** Students share their perceptions of their most important learning from a daily lesson, for example, or a unit, course, grade level, or graduation. Sample questions follow.

  ◇ What did you learn today (this week, this year)?

  ◇ What were your most important academic learnings?

  ◇ What understandings, skills, attitudes, and values have changed you and made a difference in your life? Why have these made a difference?

  ◇ What significant learning experiences stand out for you? What were they? Why do you think that they are so significant?

- **My experiences:** Students reflect on their learning experiences and share the high and low points and their growth as individuals, such as through the following.

  ◇ What do you like best about the learning experience? What would you like to change?

  ◇ Reflect on your recent learning experiences. What were the high points? The low points? How do you see yourself changing?

  ◇ What recommendations would you make to improve the learning experience in the future?

- **Individual talents and interests:** Students reflect on their own interests and talents through the following questions.

  ◇ What can you do well? What would you like to do better?

◇ Write an autobiographical statement that outlines your current strengths, talents, and interests, both inside and outside school.

- **Plans for the future:** Students consider their next steps and short- and long-term goals for the future.

  ◇ What would you like to do when you grow up?

  ◇ What could you do now to help you get there?

  ◇ Develop a plan for your future, indicating the next steps and your short- and long-term goals for the future. The plan should include research about future educational goals and career options.

Lesson Design

With a four-phase instructional model, each phase has different goals and strategies. Therefore, it becomes difficult to develop a single model or framework for each lesson. Lessons will vary depending on the instructional phase, goals, subject area, and other variables. One way to think about lesson design in a four-phase instructional context is to ask the following questions during lesson planning. These lesson-planning questions are useful at any grade level and help place a lesson into a larger four-phase framework.

- What phase of instruction dominates this lesson?

- What are the lesson goals and outcomes?

- What do you expect to accomplish at the end of the lesson?

- What is the lesson's sequence of activities? In what ways do the lesson activities engage students?

- What are the lesson's connections to previous lessons?

- What are the lesson's connections to follow-up lessons?

As a practice, complete the reproducible "Instructional Plan for a Unit of Study" (page 79).

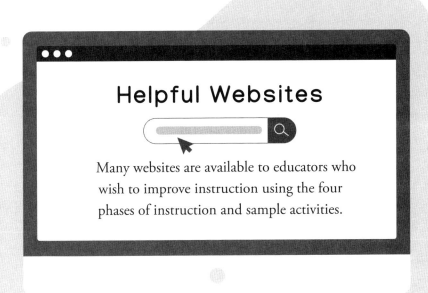

Helpful Websites

Many websites are available to educators who wish to improve instruction using the four phases of instruction and sample activities.

- "Fourteen Activators That Will Give Your Lessons Pop" (Comprehension Connection, n.d.) at **https://bit.ly/388jbC9**

- Graphic Organizer Maker at **https://bit.ly/351vGxu**

- "Interactive Notebooks: Meeting the Needs of English Language Learners" (Olivares, 2012) at **www.esc4.net/users/0205/inb_ell.pdf**

- Facing History and Ourselves: Socratic Seminar at **www.facinghistory.org/resource-library/teaching-strategies/socratic-seminar**

- Vermont Writing Collaborative: Writing for Understanding at **http://bit.ly/2ShNHkQ**

Visit **go.SolutionTree.com/21stcenturyskills** for live links to these and other resources.

Reflections—Chapter 2

The following questions and activities should provoke and stimulate thought and discussion about lifelong learning instruction.

- After reviewing the following underlying principles for lifelong learning instruction, what are their key ideas? After summarizing them, answer the following question: What might teachers do differently to put these principles into practice?

  1. Research-based learning

  2. Productive struggle and independent learning

  3. Growth and improvement through assessment and feedback

- Review the idea of learning progressions and then answer the following questions: What do learning progressions suggest for the way individual classroom instruction should be organized? How can teachers and schools develop a better progression of understandings and skills over time?

Action Steps—Chapter 2

Consider taking the following action steps to improve lifelong learning instruction.

- Use the reproducible "Lifelong Learning Instruction Recommendations" (page 78) to help you review and reflect on the major instructional ideas in this chapter. Then develop and record a brief action plan for each idea.

- Create a list of people and places who might be able to add to student learning experiences, including family members, friends, coworkers, businesses, college and university contacts, nonprofit organizations, local museums, and others. Which of these might realistically be helpful in expanding student experiences as visitors to the classroom, places to visit, and people to interview?

- Conduct further research on one activity in this chapter that interests you in the Phase-Related Instructional Strategies section (page 51). If you have the opportunity, pilot it to see how it works in the classroom. Then determine whether the activity did indeed promote the goals of lifelong learning. Consider these questions: Did the work promote a growth mindset? Were students more interested and engaged in learning? Did they build a better foundation of lifelong learning understandings and skills? Were they able to work independently or interdependently? Did their work improve?

- Use the reproducible "Instructional Plan for a Unit of Study" (page 79) to develop a four-phase instructional plan for a single unit. If possible, pilot the unit to determine its strengths and weaknesses.

Lifelong Learning Instruction Recommendations

Use this chart to help you review and reflect on the major instruction ideas in this chapter, as identified in the left column. Then, in the right column, develop and record a brief action plan for each idea.

Lifelong Learning Instruction Ideas	Action Plan Recommendations
The four-phase instructional model and related activities	
The five general lifelong learning teaching activities	
Research-based learning	
Productive struggle and independent learning	
Growth and improvement through assessment and feedback	
Learning progressions	

Instructional Plan for a Unit of Study

Develop a four-phase instructional plan for a unit of study. Briefly describe the key activities in each phase.

Unit:

Subject:

Grade level:

Instructional Phase	Instructional Plan
Setting the stage	
Building the foundation	
Deepening learning	
Providing closure	

CHAPTER 3

Assessing for
Lifelong Learning

Assessment should be more like a photo album, capturing many moments of learning. . . . If we treated assessment like a photo album, we'd use a variety of moments to get a better picture of student learning. A photo album is celebratory and powerful, and assessment should be the same.

—Andrew Miller

In this chapter I turn to the issue of assessing lifelong learning and describe how three types of assessments—(1) diagnostic, (2) formative, and (3) summative—lead to improved performance and achievement on lifelong learning goals. I can illustrate all three assessment types with the example of a child learning to ride a bike. When teaching someone how to ride a two-wheeled bike, the first thing a teacher might do is to diagnose what the learner can already do. Can he get on the bike? If there are gears, does he know how they work? This *diagnostic assessment* gives some idea where to begin the instruction.

A second type of assessment—*formative*—gives the bike rider feedback for improvement. As we begin to teach bike riding, we want to provide appropriate learning experiences, such as understanding how to get on the bike, how to use the gears, how to use the brakes, and how to turn. We give the bike rider a chance to try these things out, and as he practices and rides we want to give him the feedback he needs to help him to revise what he does and improve his bike riding over time.

Finally, when the bike rider is able to ride the bike independently, the teacher steps back and assesses riding ability and determining whether the learner still needs help. This is *summative assessment*, designed to determine whether the bike rider has mastered the skills of bike riding and met a standard of excellence—the learner can ride the bike without support, brake competently, and make turns.

While this chapter will examine many examples of diagnostic and summative assessment, I will stress the idea of formative assessment, since a major goal of lifelong learning is to foster a growth mindset—continued growth and development.

Diagnostic Assessments

Good instruction includes diagnostic assessments in advance of learning. Diagnostic assessments primarily occur while setting the stage and are designed to assist planning and enable teachers to tailor instruction to students' needs. For example, if students already have learned and remember basic information, a teacher can begin to ask open-ended questions for discussion, have students write reflective essays or create projects as a major part of the instructional process. On the other hand, if diagnostic assessments determine that students have limited background knowledge and understandings, teachers will need to spend much more time providing them with foundational knowledge, key events, and causes before more advanced thinking and writing take place.

Teachers' learning goals for students determine what diagnostic assessments they use. For example, if students already have learned and remember basic information about the American Revolution, a teacher can begin to ask open-ended questions for discussion, or have students write reflective essays or create projects as a major part of the instructional process. On the other hand, if diagnostic assessments determine that students have limited background knowledge and understandings, teachers will need to spend much more time providing foundational knowledge of the Revolution, including key events and its causes, before more advanced thinking and writing take place.

Some types of activities are specifically designed to be diagnostic for use during phase one, setting the stage. Examples of diagnostic assessments such as activators and the KWL activity were described in chapter 2 (page 41). However, an anticipation guide is another diagnostic. It reveals knowledge and understanding of a unit's key ideas prior to instruction. The anticipation guide includes a series of agree-disagree-don't know statements that students respond to, either in writing or by raising hands.

The guide also acts as a catalyst for discussion about the upcoming unit. Figure 3.1 is an example of an anticipation guide developed for a unit on the American Revolution.

Read each statement. Make a check mark in the correct column whether you agree with (A), disagree with (D), or don't know (DN) each statement. Think about why you agree or disagree with the statement, and be prepared to share your reasons.			
A	D	DN	Statement
			The American Revolution was fought to end slavery.
			Taxation without representation was a key reason for the American Revolution.
			A tax on tea was a big issue during the American Revolution.
			The American Revolution was fought against the French government.
			Tories were Americans who supported the Revolution.
			Thomas Jefferson led the Revolutionary army.
			There were twenty American colonies that fought against the British.
			The American soldiers almost lost the war.
			Americans formed a republic when the war ended instead of having a monarchy.
			After the war was over, the division between slave states and free states led to great difficulties in creating a Constitution.

Figure 3.1: Example anticipation guide developed for an American Revolution unit.

Formative Assessments

In his book, *An Ethic of Excellence: Building a Culture of Craftsmanship With Students*, Ron Berger (2003) says, "In carpentry there is no higher compliment builders give to each other than this: That guy is a *craftsman*. This one word says it all" (p. 1). Whether in sports, chess, music, theater, dance, welding, or plumbing, improving one's knowledge and skills over time, striving for excellence, and becoming an expert—a craftsperson—are what we hope to achieve. As our students work and practice, we hope that they too will continually improve their skills and ultimately become experts. How do we make that happen?

Formative assessments, used primarily in the last three phases of instruction, are designed to provide students with feedback information while they are learning and give students the opportunity to improve their work. Formative assessments also provide feedback and guidance to a teacher so that he or she knows what students have learned and then can better decide on the next teaching steps.

Formative assessments nurture a growth mindset, with which "students see mistakes as learning opportunities, and they learn from feedback. Instead of feeling like they've failed the task, students realize that they haven't met the expectations . . . yet" (Hellerich, 2020). Educator Kimberly Hellerich (2020) suggests the use of *retakes*—multiple opportunities for students to rework assignments—to foster a growth mindset. Students are given many opportunities to rework errors and earn additional credit during a two-week window.

Another way to foster formative assessments and the development of a growth mindset is to encourage peer-to-peer feedback. The positive aspects of student to student formative assessment are not only that students get feedback and guidance to improve their work, but students also learn how to critique and guide other students—and themselves—in their learning.

Different formative assessment types and formative assessment principles are discussed next.

Formative Assessment Types

Some types of instructional activities are useful for providing formative assessments. An open-ended assignment asking students to write a persuasive essay not only works as instruction but also works as a formative assessment. The students can write drafts for which the teacher (or peers) give helpful feedback. Performance tasks not only provide opportunities for significant learning and the development of life-long learning skills, but enable teachers to give feedback and coaching that improve research and writing skills.

Some formative assessments that can be used to check for understanding and improve learning follow.

- Exit slips at the end of a lesson show what students take away from a lesson. A 3-2-1 exit slip asking students to list three things they learned today, two things they found interesting, and one question reveals what students learned, how well they grasped key points, and what they need reiterated. The results of the first question (three things you learned today) can be sorted into three piles—those who got the main ideas, those who sort of got them, and those who didn't get them—to help a teacher determine what to teach next (Thomas, 2019).

- Periodic use of questions that ask students to explain a concept, retell a story in their own words, or demonstrate a solution to a problem lets teachers know what to reteach (Fisher & Frey, 2014).

- *Dipsticks* are short activities, used periodically during lessons, that check for understanding. For example, students may work in pairs to quiz each other and make sure both understand a concept. If they do, they can create a drawing or diagram to demonstrate that understanding. If they don't, they can develop a question to share with the class (Thomas, 2019).

Formative Assessment Principles

Several researchers have described research-based principles and best practices for formative assessment, among them Susan M. Brookhart (with Anthony J. Nitko, 2008) and Grant Wiggins (2012). In this book, our focus will be on five assessment principles described by educator Carol Ann Tomlinson (2012), well known for her work on differentiated instruction. These powerful principles and practical ideas were developed from her own analysis of her classroom teaching experiences and should help teachers as they implement formative assessments in the classroom. Tomlinson's (2012) five principles are as follows.

1. Develop and share core target goals.
2. Provide examples of excellent, proficient, and poor work.
3. Give precise feedback and suggest specific improvement steps.
4. Engage students in the improvement process.
5. Don't grade students during the improvement process.

Develop and Share Core Target Goals

The first step in improving learning is to develop a clear target for improvement, and to share that target with students. Unfortunately, teachers may not have a focused, targeted goal for improvement. And often, even when there is clarity, it is not shared with students. In a lifelong learning education environment, targeted goals might include improving core understandings, research, analysis, or writing skills, or applying key skills to a new situation.

Provide Examples of Excellent, Proficient, and Poor Work

Sharing and discussing poor, good, and excellent writing samples, research tools and methods, or models of good and poor thinking are powerful ways to help students understand what excellence means and what to strive for. Sometimes excellent work is found in the students' own current work or work they completed in the past. Sometimes teachers need to search for models of excellence from other sources. Sharing elements of excellence with students in a rubric format can also help students understand a teacher's expectations. (For more on rubrics, see page 94.) As Berger (2003) says:

> And so I spend my life [as a teacher] collecting good work. Most of it comes from my own [elementary] students, but I [also] gather work from other classrooms in the school and other schools I visit. When I begin a new project with my students, I go to my library of models and pin up work, show slides of work, photocopies of work, and together we admire, we critique and analyze. My students are excited to see models of everything. (p. 83)

Give Precise Feedback and Suggest Specific Improvement Steps

Two key words are here: *precise* and *specific*. Given a student's current level of work, what *precise, exacting* feedback and *specific, helpful* suggestions for next steps will help a student make improvements? For example, clearly communicating to students the elements that define excellence helps teachers transform vague and general feedback into useful, precise feedback and specific, helpful suggestions.

Engage Students in the Improvement Process

In her classes, Tomlinson (2012) asked students to write notes to her indicating "which elements of her feedback seemed useful to them and which elements seemed off target" (p. 89). The class also wrote a brief plan for how they would use the helpful feedback to improve their writing. When there were misunderstandings in interpreting her feedback, Tomlinson met with the student briefly after class to clarify. This changed the improvement process from one that was being done *to* students to one that was being done *with* students! It also customized the learning process so that students developed their own unique plan and owned the result. And, finally, by engaging students in the improvement process, students had a chance to learn how to analyze their own writing strengths and weaknesses, increasing the possibility of significant long-term results (Tomlinson, 2012).

Don't Grade Students During the Improvement Process

Tomlinson (2012) realized that her early grading of writing got in the way of student improvement: "Many [students] were so focused on getting the right answer that actual learning was a sidebar" (p. 89). So Tomlinson decided not to grade any writing until near the end of the semester. The upshot was that, during the early part of the semester, the students developed a true learning community that helped them all improve their writing. Other researchers, including education authors Jay McTighe and Ken O'Connor (2005) and Tom Schimmer (2019), as well as the National Council of Teachers of English (2013), concur.

Summative Assessments

A summative assessment occurs at the end of a specified time period, such as the end of a unit or at the end of the year. To assess summatively, teachers need to create *performance standards*—a set of expectations. Often, teachers describe their performance standards in terms of a rubric with descriptions of proficiency levels like those that follow.

1. **Beginning:** Limited mastery of essential knowledge and skills; may require assistance or extended time in applying knowledge and skills

2. **Progressing:** Partial mastery of essential knowledge and skills; partial success in tasks using knowledge or skill

3. **Proficient:** Solid academic performance, demonstrates competency of subject matter knowledge, applies such knowledge to real-world situations

4. **Advanced:** Superior performance, in-depth understanding, application of knowledge skills to develop new understanding and solutions. (O'Connor, 2002, p. 73)

Using these four levels, a teacher determines whether a student has achieved the identified learning goals. Summative assessment standards are also often used to determine grades. For example, reaching the advanced level, superior performance, might lead to a grade of A, meeting the proficient level a grade of B, and so on. Student test results on a more typical traditional final exam are also often used to determine a student's grade. For example, scores above a 90 on a test are considered superior or advanced performance and given an A, whereas an 80–99 might be considered proficient and receive a B.

In reality, a summative assessment is not necessarily the last time for assessing, and therefore is not always the end of improvement and learning. For example, there are many ways to continue improving bike riding: learning racing skills, learning to ride up and down on hills, using multiple gears appropriately, riding on different types of bikes, and so on. Formative and summative assessments may continue into the future.

Assessments That Function Formatively and Summatively

What are some key assessments that might be used to both improve learning and measure the varied achievement goals of lifelong learning? Which of these assessments are also useful and valuable instructional activities? Major types of assessments, each with different measurement strengths and weaknesses, are explained.

- Limited-response assessments
- Interactive notebooks
- Open-ended assignments
- Performance tasks and projects
- Visual learning tools
- Self-reflections
- Informal and criterion-referenced assessments

Interactive notebooks, open-ended assignments, performance tasks and projects, visual learning tools, and self-reflections are valuable instructional activities that were described in some detail in chapter 2 (page 41).

Limited-Response Assessments

Limited-response assessments (traditional or standardized assessments) consist primarily of multiple-choice, matching, labeling, and short-answer questions that require brief essays or show-your-work responses. Limited-response assessments are good for determining whether students have retained facts and can identify information correctly, and for measuring whether students can find and sort information from a predetermined set of responses and make low-level inferences. They can also help evaluate whether students are able to write coherent short essays.

When it comes to measuring key lifelong learning understandings, skills, and habits of mind, limited-response assessments have significant limitations. It is difficult to use them to assess whether students can explain key concepts, creatively organize thoughts and ideas, and explore connections and develop relationships among knowledge and data. They are not useful for determining whether students have learned how to conduct research and process information, read and understand a long text, and organize, synthesize, and interpret information and ideas in complex ways. These types of assessments don't reveal whether students can put together and discuss persuasive arguments, write and discuss an analysis of the meaning of historical events, create or critique a scientific experiment, explain how they derived their answers to a mathematical problem, write long and interesting fictional narratives, or write coherent essays and research papers. Limited-response assessments are often timed, which means that students who need extra time to process questions and information to get the right answer may do poorly on them but still know the answers. They are generally easy to grade, but the limitations of computerized grading systems and multiple-choice, short-answer questions prevent complex analyses of student work.

Although they have many limitations, several modifications can improve their ability to assess lifelong learning.

- **Think of them as a tool for mastery rather than mystery "gotcha" tests:** Unfortunately, many times limited-response assessments are designed primarily to sort students into higher-achieving and lower-achieving groups, so that some questions purposely focus on esoteric information with little meaningful context or connections to important events and ideas. Instead, these assessments should assess whether students have learned basic, foundational, important ideas, and whether students can demonstrate their ability to apply key skills. Teachers should discuss and indicate to students what will be included on such a test and give them time to learn and practice.

- **Assess understanding and higher-level skill usage:** For example, multiple-choice questions are often designed to determine whether students can recall core facts and information through many discrete, separate questions.

Each question may ask students to identify a key event during a historical period or solve a simple equation out of context. In history, students might match dates with events, with no connections to key ideas or patterns. You can improve limited-response assessments by instead using multiple-choice questions to determine whether students have developed an understanding of patterns, sequences, and key concepts. For example, instead of asking whether students can identify a single event, students might be asked to correct a sequence of events to illustrate a causal chain, or to put a series of events into a correct sequential order through a matching question of numbers and events.

- **Use them only as a formative assessment tool:** Short quizzes given throughout a unit, with preconstructed response items, are a good way to quickly assess whether students have learned key knowledge and understandings. Mid-term and final exams work as formative assessments. For example, in my own teaching, I scored limited-response assessments, returned the results to students, and then discussed the questions and answers with students so they knew the correct answers and why they were correct. I gave students the opportunity to question my answer choices and argue for another answer as correct, provided they gave evidence. In many cases, students were able to identify another answer equally as correct as mine, and therefore everyone who answered the question with the equally correct answer got additional credit for that answer. This turned out to be a very useful learning experience for students in two ways—they got to learn what I determined were the correct answers and the thinking behind them, and also had the chance to advocate for answers in ways that I had not thought of. I was able to learn more about their thinking.

Interactive Notebooks

Interactive notebooks are useful to teach students how to take notes, record, collect, and organize information in traditional formats from a teacher, text, or other resources. They also help students process information, reflect on their learning, find and summarize additional resources, develop connections and relationships, conduct analyses, synthesize data in interesting ways, solve challenges creatively, and develop persuasive arguments. In other words, students are able to organize a notebook so that, on the one hand, they collect and organize information and ideas, and, on the other hand, they analyze, synthesize, and apply information and ideas in meaningful ways.

While interactive notebooks (chapter 2) are a valuable teaching tool, they also allow a teacher to assess how much students know and understand. The notebooks can help a teacher evaluate a student's understanding of key concepts, note-taking ability, information organization, pattern finding, writing coherence, creative thinking, and so on, by reviewing the completed work in an interactive notebook. Teachers can periodically collect the notebooks to review work and provide feedback both on how to improve students' notebook use and the work generated by it. Teachers might conference with students to discuss and evaluate the completed tasks in their notebooks. Collecting the interactive notebooks at the end of a unit or term works as part of a summative assessment.

Open-Ended Assignments

As indicated in chapter 2, open-ended assignments are those that don't have a single correct answer and that allow students to develop their own original approach, process, or product. They are designed to create new ways of thinking about problems and challenges, allow alternative possibilities and options, and enable innovative thinking.

Examples of open-ended assignments include when students are asked to do the following.

- Explain a historical event in your own words.
- Suggest various ways to solve a mathematical problem.
- Create your own analysis of a graph.
- Draw your own conclusion from a scientific experiment.
- Interpret a piece of writing, such as an essay, book, or other primary source.
- Develop your own responses to a question posed in a foreign language.
- Write a persuasive essay arguing for a point of view on a controversial topic.
- Develop your own interpretive artwork or musical composition.
- Write an essay or reflective piece in a format and style of your own choosing.
- Write an original poem on a topic being studied.
- Express your final thoughts and reflections on a unit topic in a written or visual format.

Open-ended assignments also enable teachers to assess whether students have reached a level of expertise that demonstrates successful achievement—a summative assessment. For example, comparing a student's response to an open-ended assignment, one given before a unit and one given after a unit, is useful as a measure of student growth, and the comparison can function as a summative assessment.

Performance Tasks and Projects

Performance tasks and projects (chapter 2, and chapter 5, page 137) are not only important teaching tools but also important for assessing lifelong learning. They:

> Allow teachers to gather information about what students can actually do with what they are learning—science experiments that students design, carry out, analyze, and write up; computer programs that students create and test out; research inquiries that they pursue, assembling evidence about a question that they present in written and oral form. Whether the skill or standard being measured is writing, speaking, scientific or mathematical literacy, or knowledge of history and social science research, students actually perform tasks involving these skills and the teacher or other rater scores the performance based upon a set of pre-determined criteria. (Darling-Hammond & Adamson, 2010, p. 8)

A key way to use performance tasks and projects as assessments is to develop and share rubrics with students. (You can further explore rubrics in chapter 5.) Projects and performance tasks assess whether students have learned specific understandings and skills at various transition levels, such as from one grade level to another, from one course to another, from primary to upper elementary, upper elementary to middle school, and middle school to high school. Capstone projects assess student learning at graduation. For example, a transition or capstone assessment project, designed to measure scientific understanding, might require students to read a scientific experiment from which they must draw conclusions about its accuracy, biases, replicability, and significance.

The following student skills are commonly assessed when someone works on a project or performance task, for instance.

- Organize and manage learning.

- Develop essential questions and challenges.

- Conduct research.

- Organize knowledge and form patterns.

- Creatively solve problems.

- Work in groups.

- Write a research paper, essay, persuasive argument, or op-ed piece.

- Demonstrate understanding through the creation of a poster, diagram, plan, film, or podcast.

- Participate effectively in discussions.

- Create and make presentations to others.

Visual Learning Tools

In chapter 2, I examined how visual learning tools can improve learning. Here I explore how to use visual learning tools for both formative and summative assessments. These tools enable students to visually represent ideas and relationships and enable teachers to assess whether students can display their understandings and ideas visually (Hyerle, 2009; McTighe & Silver, 2020).

One type of visual learning tool—mind maps—is useful for both formative and summative assessment. Mind maps give students the opportunity to organize their "thoughts around a central idea," representing their thinking at a given point, so teachers can "get a full picture at a glance and see what is missing" (Tanguay, 2020). They "offer students 'think time' for showing what they know in an interrelated form so that teachers can quickly review their webs" (Hyerle, 2009, p. 64). In mind mapping, teachers provide students with a sheet of paper that only has a central circle that has a topic or key concept in it. Students create a map to show their understanding and thinking about that topic or concept, with lines depicting relationships.

Self-Reflections

Self-reflections provide students with the opportunity to share their perceptions of what they have learned, discuss their self-development and growth as learners and individuals, and share their plans for the future. By creating personal perspectives, explanations, and interpretations, students reveal their comprehension and a variety of lifelong learning skills. As described in chapter 2, multiple types of self-reflections function as both instruction and assessment.

- Academic learning

- Academic experiences

- Individual talents and interests

- Plans for the future

An additional example of a self-reflection assessment is one developed by the Educational Testing Service (1993) and adapted for this book. This letter-writing assessment activity, given as a culminating activity, is designed to challenge students to write or draw about a unit they have just completed. The task is to write a letter to someone who is important to you explaining the key elements of the unit just completed. The students discuss what they learned and how they will use what they have learned in other situations. Students may also include questions they still have that were not answered during the unit. Another example is when each student develops a personal concept map—a visual diagram of interconnected terms and ideas learned from a unit—and shares it with the teacher and other students at the end of a unit. The personal concept map can accompany a statement explaining how the ideas in the concept map are relevant to the student's personal life or to the world at large.

Informal and Criterion-Referenced Assessments

Several additional types of assessments—informal and criterion referenced—are useful as formative and summative assessments. For example, during classroom discussions, teachers might listen for the quality of individual student comments and observe how students listen and respond to others. Observing students as they work on projects and assignments, and how they work with others in groups, is also helpful. Criterion-referenced tests are useful for evaluating progress toward specific objectives, such as improved reading skills, and measuring reading levels.

Rubrics

How do teachers measure success and achievement when using the types of complex assessments described in this book? One solution is to create rubrics. According to education author Susan M. Brookhart (2013), a rubric is "a coherent set of criteria for students' work that includes descriptions of levels of performance quality on the criteria" (p. 1). Another definition is an:

> established criterion for assessing the mastery of outlined skills and/or content. To state this more simply, a rubric shows you what an assignment would look like if it were done right, and also what it would look like if there were areas that needed improvement. (Stanley, 2019, p. 9)

A rubric combines multiple criteria for success with levels of achievement and is often used as a way to provide feedback so students can improve their work and move on to a higher level of achievement. This evaluative and feedback tool describes the criteria for and characteristics of good work, with each criterion or characteristic usually broken down in terms of levels of excellence.

Consider the assessment of a student's ability to effectively write a persuasive essay. What criteria might measure success? According to Judith Arter and Jay McTighe (2001), the writer should show evidence of achievement on the following persuasive writing:

- A well-written opinion
- Effective use of evidence
- Coherent development of an argument
- Inclusion of counterarguments rebutted in the essay (p. 129)

Figure 3.2 (page 96) is an example of a rubric for evaluating a persuasive essay using these characteristics. Rubrics have many uses.

- They help students to understand what is expected of them. Students can discuss the criteria embedded in a rubric when the teacher introduces a task. Teachers can also introduce examples of good and poor work to illustrate the criteria during this discussion.

- They can provide students with feedback on how well they have achieved the criteria for success, so they have the opportunity to improve their work.

- They can function as a summative assessment, rating how well students have successfully completed a task.

Chapter 5 (page 137) has more information about developing and using rubrics.

Portfolios

What is a *portfolio*? One definition asserts that it "is a purposeful collection and sampling of student work that exhibits a student's efforts, progress, and achievements in one or more areas" (Paulson, Paulson, & Meyer, 1991, p. 60). This definition articulates an important point about portfolios: they are not just a collection of assessments to be used for grading isolated pieces of work but also a way to comprehensively assess a student's overall growth and achievement.

	Emerging	Developing	Proficient	Advanced
Opinion statement	Few elements included and done well	Some elements included and a few done well	Most elements included and done well	All elements included and done well
	No opinion statement included	Opinion statement included, but poorly written, unclear, or confusing	Opinion statement included, but needs more precision and clarity	Clear, coherent opinion statement with clear definitions and explanations
Use of evidence	No evidence included	Little evidence, poorly integrated into the essay	Good evidence examples used, but not always enough information and data	Uses excellent examples of evidence, with clear information and data to support it
Coherent argument	No coherence or organization	Some coherence, but often confusing and disjointed	Often coherent, but sometimes confusing and disjointed	Highly coherent and well organized
Rebuttal of counterarguments	No counterarguments	Occasionally uses counterarguments, but not often integrated into the essay	Illustrates counterarguments often, with good rebuttals to the counterarguments	A well-organized set of counterarguments and rebuttals well integrated into the essay

Figure 3.2: Rubric for writing a persuasive essay.

Over the course of a year or several years of schooling, selected results from a variety of assessment types and student work can go into a portfolio for a comprehensive picture of a student's levels of learning and growth.

Developing Portfolios

The portfolio process begins with deciding what students will include in a portfolio and how the portfolio system will work. Some helpful questions follow.

- How can the goals of a lifelong learning education—developing a growth mindset, ongoing development of understandings and skill sets, deep and independent learning, broad and enriched learning—be helpful in deciding what to collect in a portfolio?

- What types of assessments might students place into portfolios?

- What student writing belongs in a portfolio? Essays? Interpretations of literature? Fictional works? Poetry? Summaries? Research reports? Other?

- Should portfolios include performance tasks and projects?

- Do student self-reflections belong in a portfolio?

- Should portfolios showcase the best work only or the same types of work over time showing progress and growth?

- How will student work be collected? Organized? Reviewed? Are there existing folders of student work that might become collections that illustrate growth over time?

Once teachers determine the portfolio content, they can then place much of the effort of both collecting and sorting portfolio work into the hands of students. Students can form the habit of placing their work into portfolios. At designated times, teachers can ask students to purge their portfolios or to showcase only their best work. Students can also write periodic self-reflections to include in their portfolios that indicate how they feel about the progress they have made and their portfolio goals for the future. This way of handling portfolios also supports the development of student self-management and self-reflection skills.

With internet capability, students can digitally create, scan, and place their work into electronic portfolios. Educator and school principal Matt Renwick's (2017) *Digital Portfolios in the Classroom: Showcasing and Assessing Student Work* provides a good introduction to the development and use of this assessment tool as a teaching and learning innovation.

The results of using portfolios in schools and classrooms may be surprising in ways not anticipated.

- The collection and analysis of written student work over time, coupled with teacher and peer feedback, should have a significant effect on the quality of the work, and might help significantly improve reading and writing skills.

- Teachers may find it helpful to meet in teams to analyze portfolio results across disciplines and grade levels and discover what students can do well and what they need to improve. The results of this analysis can lead to teacher teams working more closely together to improve student learning.

- School leaders might find it useful to collect and share portfolio assessment data and examples of student work with the general public in order to wean the community away from solely using test scores as the instruments to best measure school and district success. For example, some teachers might demonstrate at a board meeting how they use portfolios to collect, organize, and evaluate student learning over time.

Presenting Portfolios

Portfolios work as assessment for and sharing of an individual's nuanced and varied skill levels, talents, abilities, and interests. For example, a teacher, student, and parent or guardian can discuss a student's portfolio at conferences to evaluate and reflect on the quality of work and progress. A graduation portfolio presentation in front of a panel of educators and community representatives enables students to present their work, answer questions, and get feedback from the panel on their strengths and challenges.

The following are some examples of questions that teachers might ask students during a portfolio conference and presentation.

- "How does this portfolio represent you—your strengths, challenges, interests, and talents?"

- "What have you learned through the process of completing and collecting the items in your portfolio?"

- "What are your strongest academic skills? What are your challenges and problem areas?"

- "What have been your most important academic learnings and why?"

- "How does your portfolio illustrate your growth as a student? As a whole person?"

- "What do you now see as your greatest strengths? What are your interests and talents?"

- "What are your next steps? What are your plans for the future?"

Assessment Principles

Keeping in mind when to employ the three assessment categories—(1) diagnostic, (2) formative, and (3) summative—coupled with the use of portfolios, provides a comprehensive assessment framework for lifelong learning. This way of thinking about assessments can be summarized and synthesized through the following assessment principles.

- Create a powerful assessment process.

- Create mastery, not mystery, assessments.

- Treat assessment as a friend, as an "act of love."

Create a Powerful Assessment Process

Diagnostic, formative, and summative assessments, along with portfolios, in some combination with each other, can create a powerful multilayered lifelong learning assessment process at any level and in any subject area. For example, using an appropriate mix of the key types of lifelong learning assessments described in this chapter is more likely to assess key lifelong learning skills, such as the ability to form patterns, explain key ideas and theories, and conduct research. A mix of several types of assessments will help to evaluate complex skills accurately. Portfolios not only provide opportunities to collect student work and showcase that work, but also vividly illustrate growth over time.

Create Mastery, Not Mystery, Assessments

One way of thinking about the assessments used to determine success in sports, music, biking, and the arts is that they are designed to create *mastery* rather than *mystery*. The knowledge and skills needed for success are transparent to everyone. Models of success are all around. For example, everyone who plays basketball knows what successful players do by observing them and learning from coaches.

Unfortunately, in many classrooms, mastery assessments are often not the norm. Rather, mystery often surrounds classroom assessments. What's going to be on the test? Did my teacher give me enough information to prepare? How well can I prepare if I don't know what's going to be included? Will there be "trick" questions? Making tests more mastery friendly and transparent should be the rule rather than the exception. Providing students with clear indications of what will be on the test; providing models of successful work; creating open-book, untimed tests; creating and sharing rubrics—all of these promote a mastery approach to learning.

Treat Assessment as a Friend, as an "Act of Love"

In a commentary on assessment, English teacher Christina Torres (2019) discusses how assessment data are not just "cold-hearted tools that reduce . . . students to weaknesses and numbers, [but also] can be another way . . . to . . . build deeper and more loving connections with students" (p. 2). Instead of tools that show student deficiencies, assessments can "ensure we are giving students the tools and skills they need and perhaps even to look for the gifts they bring to the table" (Torres, 2019). A healthy relationship with assessment means students perceive them as providing opportunity for self-reflection and growth. Sharing that understanding—part of building a growth mindset and positive, strong relationships with students—helps students see how to use data to improve one's learning.

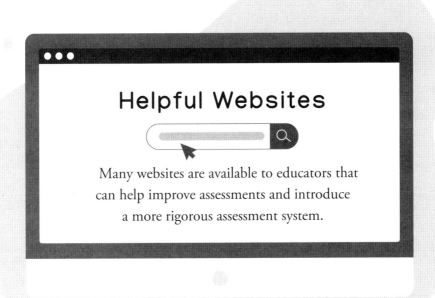

Helpful Websites

Many websites are available to educators that
can help improve assessments and introduce
a more rigorous assessment system.

- "6 Best Mind Mapping Tools for Creative Students" (Meiser, 2016) at **https://bit.ly/2JC43TY**

- *Education Week*: Projects, Portfolios, and Performance Assessments at **https://tinyurl.com/y2dc8p7d**

- Learning Policy Institute: California Performance Assessment Collaborative at **https://bit.ly/3n8f4ua**

- MC2STEM High School Capstone Design Process at **https://sites.google.com/a/mc2stemhs.net/capstone-design-process**

- New York Performance Standards Consortium at **www.performanceassessment.org**

- Performance Assessment Resource Bank at **www.performanceassessmentresourcebank.org**

- RubiStar at **http://rubistar.4teachers.org/index.php**

Visit **go.SolutionTree.com/21stcenturyskills** for
live links to these and other resources.

Reflections—Chapter 3

The following questions and activities should provoke and stimulate thought and discussion about lifelong learning assessment.

- Chapter 3 focuses on using diagnostic, formative, and summative assessments to support student growth and achievement. How might these three types of assessment work in a sport, game, or art education experience?

- Review the section (page 88) that describes how to improve limited-response assessments for measuring complex lifelong learning goals and how they can function as formative assessments. What other ways could you change them to better measure lifelong learning goals? Decide which suggestions you might implement.

- This chapter and chapter 2 (page 41) suggest that five types of activities—(1) interactive notebooks, (2) open-ended assignments, (3) performance tasks and projects, (4) visual learning tools, and (5) self-reflections—are useful as both instructional activities and assessments. How would you rank them according to their usefulness and importance for both instruction and assessment? Reflect on how the highest-ranking activities might be best integrated into classroom and school settings.

- Review the section in this chapter on portfolios (page 95). Brainstorm how portfolios might be helpful in measuring lifelong learning and student growth.

- Reflect on how the lifelong learning assessment principles described in this chapter help you think about assessments in a different way, and what the implications are for the use of lifelong learning assessments in the classroom.

  ◇ Create a powerful assessment process.

  ◇ Create mastery, not mystery, assessments.

  ◇ Treat assessment as a friend, as an "act of love." (Torres, 2019)

Action Steps—Chapter 3

Consider taking the following action steps to improve lifelong learning assessment.

- Decide which assessments described in this chapter you would most likely use to measure achievement of key understandings, lifelong learning skills, and a growth mindset. Which would work best for you, and why? Make a plan as to how you would incorporate these assessments into a classroom or school situation.

- Review the main assessment types described in this chapter. Then, using the reproducible "Audit of Current Assessments" (page 104), list your current use of each assessment, the pluses for using each assessment, the minuses of using each, and what's interesting about the assessment idea. In the final column, suggest how you might use each assessment in the future. If you are currently teaching, create a plan to institute any of these changes in the future.

- Consider whether portfolios are a viable option for a classroom or school. If yes, make a plan to begin using them or to improve their use.

Audit of Current Assessments

Use this chart to analyze your current use of each assessment, the pluses and minuses for using each assessment, the interesting points about each assessment, and how you might use each assessment in the future.

	Current Use	Pluses for Using Each Assessment Type	Minuses for Using Each Assessment Type	Interesting Points About Each Assessment Type	Future Use of Each Assessment Type
Limited-Response Assessments					
Interactive Notebooks					
Open-Ended Assignments					
Performance Tasks and Projects					
Visual Learning Tools					
Self-Reflections					
Criterion-Referenced Tests					
Informal Assessments					

Teaching for Lifelong Learning © 2021 Elliott Seif • SolutionTree.com

Visit **go.SolutionTree.com/21stcenturyskills** to download this free reproducible.

CHAPTER 4

Developing a Lifelong Learning Curriculum

Implementing a coherent, content-rich curriculum may be the most foundational element of effective schooling and has the greatest impact on students' learning, reading ability, and life chances. Yet such a curriculum is rarely created, implemented, or even monitored in the majority of our schools.

—Mike Schmoker

Like an architectural blueprint provides the structural plans for a building, a curriculum provides the structural plans for what and how students will learn. It establishes teaching goals and the year-to-year, month-to-month, week-to-week, day-to-day framework and plans for teaching, learning, and assessment. It can be superficial, impractical, and unused, or it can be supportive, helpful, and extremely useful for everyday, long-term instruction. Although the development of a powerful, focused core curriculum is critical to good teaching and learning (Marzano, 2003; Schmoker, 2018), many teachers don't work with a relevant, well-organized, teacher-friendly, effective curriculum that has appropriate goals and units designed for lifelong learning (Mehta & Fine, 2019; Wexler, 2019b).

How do we fix this problem? In many schools and districts, teachers are given the time and opportunity to map their current curriculum, select new curricula, or redesign the curriculum. This chapter will focus on how individuals or teams of teachers, administrators, curriculum directors, and others in a school or district can use that time and opportunity to design a lifelong learning curriculum.

Curriculum Characteristics That Promote Lifelong Learning

Clearly, a curriculum that is focused around lifelong learning goals and is useful, practical, and meaningful to both teachers and students is critical. How to make this happen? First and foremost, there is a need to identify a key set of curriculum characteristics for analyzing, selecting, or designing a lifelong learning curriculum. The following list and brief descriptions of twelve curriculum characteristics, which I developed from my own experience as a teacher and curriculum director, provide the key criteria for this process. In my view, a lifelong learning curriculum does the following.

1. Focuses learning around a core set of understandings, big ideas, and essential questions
2. Actively engages students and develops student curiosity and interest
3. Integrates the learning and practice of key lifelong learning skills
4. Organizes instruction to support lifelong learning education goals
5. Includes varied and valid assessments
6. Provides opportunities to build on previous learnings, learn from helpful feedback, and grow learning over time
7. Promotes coherence and learning progressions
8. Includes many types of materials and resources, including technology
9. Takes into account diverse student abilities, interests, and needs
10. Encourages interdisciplinary connections
11. Builds in outside and authentic learning experiences
12. Is well organized and easy to use

Focuses Learning Around a Core Set of Understandings, Big Ideas, and Essential Questions

Research shows that a focused curriculum that separates core learning from supplemental learning is key to achievement (Marzano, 2003; Schmoker, 2018). A lifelong learning curriculum is organized around this less-is-more approach to content. Each part of the curriculum focuses on a few key elements that allow a teacher to eliminate extraneous content and create opportunities for foundational and deeper learning. Unfortunately, many typical curriculum materials contain long lists of content goals and objectives. These objectives often fragment lessons and units. Some curricula also incorporate what they call *essential questions*, but these questions instead often focus on factual information and low-level generalizations.

To determine whether the curriculum is well focused, look for the following.

- The extent to which the curriculum identifies a limited number of big ideas—concepts, themes, issues, and understandings—that promote student understanding

- A few provocative essential questions tied to big ideas that drive interest and learning

- Big ideas and essential questions that truly focus what students study and learn

- Whether identified big ideas and essential questions are aligned with suggested activities and assessments

Actively Engages and Develops Student Curiosity and Interest

One measure of a powerful, lifelong learning curriculum is whether the student activities promote student curiosity and interest in learning. Based on the characteristics of the activities suggested in chapter 2 (page 51), along with the four underlying principles of lifelong learning instruction (page 47), here are some things to look for in the curriculum.

- The activities promote active engagement and interest in what students are learning.

- The curriculum is organized around exploring provocative and interesting essential questions (page 23).

- A research-based learning approach helps students find interest and value in learning, use multiple sources, and define and explore problems and challenges.

- The activities challenge students and lead to productive struggle and greater student independence (page 48).

Integrates the Learning and Practice of Key Lifelong Learning Skills

A lifelong learning curriculum asks students to learn, practice, and use a few key lifelong learning skills, such as those described in chapter 1 (page 30). The curriculum should emphasize learning one or more of these key skills and prioritize and heighten students' ability to do the following.

- **Develop understanding:** Make connections, find and create patterns, and develop explanations.

- **Research and inquire:** Ask good questions; search through and learn from a variety of texts; read and study well; and find, evaluate, and process information and ideas.

- **Think at high levels:** Analyze, interpret, create, and solve problems.

- **Communicate effectively:** Write coherently, speak well, and listen to others.

- **Collaborate:** Work well together in small groups.

- **Apply:** Transfer learning to new situations.

Look for the following.

- These skills are given priority in the curriculum and are continually embedded into the curriculum through both instructional strategies and assessments.

- There are continual opportunities for students to learn, practice, and deepen lifelong learning skill areas, including those that foster understanding, researching and inquiring well, thinking critically and creatively, communicating effectively, collaborating well, and demonstrating understanding by applying and transferring learning to new situations.

Organizes Instruction to Support Lifelong Learning Education Goals

Examine the curriculum materials to determine how instruction is organized. Is it the same as or similar to the four phases? If not, here are some things to look for in the curriculum.

- The ways instructional plans enable teachers to diagnose for prior knowledge and skills

- The ways instructional plans promote interest and curiosity in learning

- The ways instructional plans provide a larger context for learning

- How foundational understandings, skills, and a growth mindset are integrated into the instructional sequence

- How instructional plans refine, enlarge, and extend understanding and skills, enable independent work, and promote deep learning

- How closure—completion and sharing of student work, as well as further learning—is incorporated into instructional plans

Includes Varied and Valid Assessments

As described in chapter 3 (page 81), thoughtful open-ended assessments, interactive notebooks, performance tasks and projects, self-reflective activities, and informal assessments are important to include as part of a lifelong learning assessment approach. Look at the curriculum materials to determine the following.

- The variety of and balance between limited-response (page 88) and other assessments, such as open-ended assignments, interactive notebooks, performance tasks and projects, self-reflection activities, and visual assessments

- The validity of the assessments, particularly the links between the assessments and the goals and content of the curriculum

- The capacity for assessments to help students apply and transfer learning in order to demonstrate understanding

Provides Opportunities to Build on Previous Learnings, Learn From Helpful Feedback, and Grow Learning Over Time

Effective curricula provide multiple opportunities not only to assess students' prior knowledge and skills but also to use formative assessments to provide students with specific feedback to improve learning (chapter 3). For example, does the curriculum include student activities designed to diagnose prior understanding of key concepts and ideas in an upcoming unit? Once a teacher understands students' prior learning, does the curriculum suggest ways to integrate new and prior learning? The curriculum should also incorporate many opportunities for formative assessment.

Look for the following.

- Diagnostic assessments are included that suggest ways to measure and build on previous learning.

- Formative assessments are included that provide students with helpful feedback to improve their learning and work.

- Time is included in curriculum plans for students to examine feedback and for improving student work.

Promotes Coherence and Learning Progressions

A coherent curriculum is carefully sequenced to enable students to develop a growth mindset and to deepen understandings and use of skills over a period of time. Revisiting and refining learning over time is often called a *learning progression*. For example, a highly effective mathematics curriculum examines spatial relationships in increasingly complex ways as the year progresses. A good history textbook will examine the same big idea, such as the principles of a market economy, through multiple chapters to enhance and refine student understanding and make more complex connections.

To determine whether the curriculum is coherent and promotes learning progressions, look for the following.

- A carefully sequenced set of activities that fosters increased understanding and skill development over time.

- The same ideas and skills are purposefully revisited and developed in increasingly complex ways.

- Skills and a growth mindset are practiced, developed, and refined over time.

Includes Many Types of Materials and Resources, Including Technology

Suggested and incorporated resources and materials in a curriculum (for example, readings, podcasts, and videos) can support a research-based instructional approach (Jacobs, 2010b; Jacobs & Alcock, 2017; Seif, 1998). For example, a lifelong learning–oriented curriculum should include supplied or referenced supplemental materials that enable students to read and research many sources of information, ideas, and data. If there is no text, are there varied types of resources and materials that guide learning? Do multiple materials increase the possibility of research-based learning, open-ended assignments, and higher levels of thinking?

Also, technology can be a helpful tool for implementing a lifelong learning curriculum. Are students able to utilize meaningful technology in their learning and assessment activities? Does the curriculum contain suggested websites and other technological options within the program that provide a meaningful expansion of the teaching and learning experience?

Look for the following.

- Whether there are multiple, varied resources, such as readings, articles, videos, and podcasts incorporated into the curriculum materials that allow for thoughtful research, reading, learning, inquiry, and thinking
- Appropriate technology is incorporated to support the curriculum's goals.

Takes into Account Diverse Student Abilities, Interests, and Needs

Effective curriculum materials support the varied needs of students in a diverse classroom environment. An effective teacher's guide specifically notes differentiated strategies for various ability levels, including choices and options, modifications, accommodations for varied learners, and appropriate enrichment activities. Students with all types of special needs are capable of working with the materials at an independent level or with support from classroom teachers, special education teachers, or paraprofessionals.

Look for the following.

- How the curriculum includes modifications, accommodations, and enrichment activities that support varied needs in a diverse classroom environment, including students with special needs and English learners
- How the curriculum provides students with choices and options, such as individual research opportunities, independent projects, reading choices, and enrichment options

Encourages Interdisciplinary Connections

Lifelong learning curriculum materials encourage interdisciplinary connections. For example, curriculum materials may incorporate big ideas and essential questions that not only relate to the discipline being studied but are also useful to other disciplines as well. For example, history texts might incorporate many big ideas and essential questions about economics, government, geography, science, and health (How did science discoveries and technology inventions affect a nation during X period in history?, for example) and also reference and include aligned literature.

Science materials may include big ideas and essential questions that integrate various science disciplines, such as biology, chemistry, and physics, and suggest mathematical connections and connections to larger societal issues such as climate change. Interdisciplinary connections are also developed through the integration of the same skills and habits of mind into many subjects, such as the integration of research and investigation skills, critical and creative thinking, and writing development.

Look for the following.

- Ways the curriculum supports and encourages interdisciplinary connections by integrating big ideas and essential questions across subjects
- Interdisciplinary resources and materials
- The integration of key lifelong learning skills across disciplines

Builds In Outside and Authentic Learning Experiences

Outside and authentic learning experiences include field trips, interviews, real-life problem-solving activities, analysis of real data, and other similar experiences. The curriculum should also recognize the family's educational role. It should also include activities for parents and guardians who wish to help their children succeed and provide and extend supplemental learning experiences.

Look for the following.

- Authentic learning experiences beyond the classroom as an ongoing part of the curriculum activities
- Opportunities for parents and guardians to help their children and provide supplemental learning experiences
- Supplemental materials, such as study guides, should be available to help students, parents, and guardians understand the subject, help adults assist their children with their work, discuss together real-world issues, and continually practice and build critical lifelong learning skills.

Is Well Organized and Easy to Use

Since teachers have so many professional functions and limited time available for understanding the curriculum, it's important that curriculum materials be well organized. Teachers should be able to understand, find, and use the units, lessons, assessments, and supporting materials in a relatively easy fashion, and should be able to adapt them where necessary.

- Goals are clearly stated and focused throughout the curriculum, with units, assessments, instructional plans, and strategies clearly developed and organized around the goals.

- The time provided for implementing each unit and lesson is realistic and doable.

- Suggested outside materials are easily accessible.

- The curriculum is easily adapted to a teacher's style.

- Professional development resources required to implement the curriculum are readily available.

Three Ways to Use Lifelong Learning Characteristics to Improve the Curriculum

Teachers who wish to move their curriculum to one that promotes lifelong learning can use the twelve characteristics and their indicators to do the following.

- Analyze the current curriculum, decide where it is wanting, and then prioritize and make changes to the curriculum that improve it.

- Select and adopt a lifelong learning–friendly curriculum.

- Modify the curriculum using the UbD framework.

Analyze the Current Curriculum Against the Characteristics of a Lifelong Learning Curriculum

The first step in analyzing the current curriculum is to determine whether it meets the preceding twelve characteristics. To determine if a curriculum is consistent with the lifelong learning characteristics, use the reproducible "Curriculum Rating System" (page 123). If the current curriculum is not clearly developed or organized, it may be necessary to first map the curriculum before rating it by answering the following questions.

- **Knowledge and skill goals:** What knowledge, understandings, and skills are students expected to learn and practice?

- **Assessments:** What assessments are currently in use?

- **Instruction:** How is instruction organized? What are the key resources and materials used for instruction?

- **Curriculum flow:** What is the sequence of the curriculum at each grade level? Across grade levels? For each subject? For the year? (Jacobs, 1997; Jacobs & Johnson, 2009)

Select and Adopt a Lifelong Learning–Friendly Curriculum

If the current curriculum does not have many of the characteristics, selecting and adopting new curricula is another avenue for change. The reproducible "Curriculum Rating System" (page 123) can help systematically analyze curriculum materials in consideration for adoption.

Modify the Curriculum Using Understanding by Design

Another option for making the curriculum more consistent with a lifelong learning approach is to thoughtfully redesign it using Understanding by Design (Wiggins & McTighe, 2011). This teacher-friendly curriculum model creates curriculum courses and units through a three-stage process that (1) identifies desired results, (2) chooses key assessments, and (3) forms a learning plan (Wiggins & McTighe, 2011).

The more specific UbD design components make it consistent with the lifelong learning characteristics. For example, UbD emphasizes developing curricula around a few key understandings and essential questions (McTighe & Wiggins, 2013; Wiggins & McTighe, 2011). UbD includes a method to identify key processes and skills. It emphasizes the use of multiple assessments, including open-ended assignments, authentic performance tasks, and self-reflections, that are designed to assess understanding and lifelong learning skills (Wiggins & McTighe, 2011). You can easily incorporate the four-phase instructional model into UbD. Figure 4.1 illustrates how teachers can use the UbD template, with descriptors for each section that reflect lifelong learning characteristics, to design lifelong learning curriculum units and courses.

Stage One: Desired Results		
Established Goals	**Transfer**	
[What specific standards statements and other sources of desired results will help develop stage-one desired results?]	*Students will be able to independently use their learning to:* [What are one or a few long-term results that transcend this unit and connect to others? What are those that relate to broad, large, lifelong learning goals?]	
	Meaning	
	Understandings	**Essential Questions**
	Students will understand that: [What are one, two, or three key understandings that will be the focus of teaching and learning during this unit?]	[What are one, two, or three thought-provoking questions that will foster understanding, inquiry, meaning making, and transfer?]
	Acquisition	
	Students will know: [What key information and basic concepts are critical for understanding, and for answering the essential questions?]	*Students will be skilled at:* [Which of the lifelong learning skills and skill areas will be emphasized and taught in this unit?]
Stage Two: Evidence		
Evaluative Criteria	**Assessment Evidence**	
[For open-ended assignments and performance tasks and projects, what evaluative criteria will judge successful student work and provide feedback on work quality?]	[What open-ended assignments, used as assessments, will be given during this unit? What authentic tasks and projects will students use to demonstrate understanding and skill development?]	
[If appropriate for other evidence: What evaluative criteria will be used to judge successful student work?]	Other Evidence: [What other evidence, such as visual organizers, interactive notebooks, tests, quizzes, and self-reflections, will be collected during the unit to determine whether stage-one goals were achieved?]	

Figure 4.1: UbD unit template with lifelong learning descriptors.   *continued* →

Stage Three: Learning Plan
Summary of key learning events and instruction, including diagnostic and formative assessments

Setting the **Stage**
[What interactive activities will help do the following? • Develop student interest and curiosity • Create a context for learning • Share, develop, and explore meaningful goals with students • Introduce open-ended assignments, projects, and performance tasks • Diagnose, discover, and activate background knowledge and skills that students already have]

Building the **Foundation**
[What interactive activities do the following? • Provide students with a basic foundation of knowledge, understandings, skills, and habits of mind critical for developing unit goals • Provide feedback to improve learning and work • Foster productive struggle and help students take responsibility for their learning]

Deepening **Learning**
[What activities will help students do the following? • Develop a deeper understanding of key concepts and ideas • Independently continue practicing key skills and habits of mind • Further develop and improve their learning and work • Productively struggle • Take responsibility for their learning]

Providing **Closure**
[How will students do the following? • Complete their learning and work • Share their learning and work with others • Demonstrate and explain what they have learned • Continue their learning in the future]

Additional Resources

Source: Adapted from Wiggins & McTighe, 2011.

*Visit **go.SolutionTree.com/21stcenturyskills** for a free reproducible version of this figure.*

Unit Redesign With UbD

Redesigning and planning a unit of study using the UbD format begin with the end in mind, including outcomes and required learning evidence (Wiggins & McTighe, 2011). UbD has the following stages for unit planning, and "specific lessons are then developed in the context of a more comprehensive unit design" (Wiggins & McTighe, 2011, p. 7). The three stages of planning are as follows.

1. Identifying lifelong learning goals

2. Identifying key assessments

3. Planning instruction

The next sections will briefly walk you through the characteristics of each of the three stages, with three sample UbD units to follow. A more detailed description of the UbD unit development process appears in *The Understanding by Design Guide to Creating High-Quality Units* (Wiggins & McTighe, 2011).

Unit Planning Stage One: Identifying Lifelong Learning Goals

In order to plan a unit of study, a teacher or team of teachers does the following.

- Determines key starting points for helping to develop lifelong learning goals—for example, standards documents, textbooks, and other resources

- Develops one, or very few, powerful and meaningful big ideas, enduring understandings, and essential questions that will focus the unit (figure 1.1, page 25)

- Identifies the core knowledge students need to learn and ties them to the questions and understandings developed in the preceding step

- Identifies core skills and habits of mind for students to learn and practice, based on lifelong learning skill areas

- Describes *transfer goals*—long-term goals that can be the focus of other units and subjects

Remember—to be essential, questions should do one or more of the following (page 25).

- Require broad understanding

- Raise important ideas at the heart of a discipline

- Raise important personal questions or interdisciplinary ideas

- Provoke and stimulate thinking

- Potentially recur

Unit Planning Stage Two: Identifying Key Assessments

In stage two of the UbD planning model, teachers or teacher teams identify multiple and varied types of assessments that will help to measure lifelong learning achievements (McTighe & Wiggins, 2013). The assessments are designed to ensure that students have developed foundational knowledge and understanding, skills, and habits of mind, as well as the ability to delve more deeply and independently into learning. The following lifelong learning assessments, discussed and explored in chapter 3 (page 81), can be incorporated into the unit.

- Limited-response assessments and quizzes

- Interactive notebooks

- Open-ended assignments

- Performance tasks and projects

- Self-reflections

- Criterion-referenced tests

- Informal assessments, such as observations during group work

Teachers or teacher teams can also decide whether to use portfolios as part of the unit assessment process.

Unit Planning Stage Three: Planning Instruction

In stage three of UbD unit planning, the individual teacher or teaching team organizes instruction and describes instructional activities. One way to best meet the goals of lifelong learning is to plan those instructional activities around the four phases of instruction: (1) setting the stage, (2) building the foundation, (3) deepening learning, and (4) providing closure (page 43). Stage three of unit planning is also the place to build in opportunities to diagnose and expand on previous learning, to build curiosity and interest in what is to be learned, to indicate how formative assessments will be included, to teach from a variety of activities that engage students and enable them to productively struggle and take responsibility for their own learning, and to modify instruction to take into account diverse student interests and needs.

Three sample units appear as reproducible examples.

- "Citizenship Unit for Elementary School Students" (page 125)
- "Science Unit for Middle School Students" (page 129)
- "Poetry Unit for High School Students" (page 133)

Curriculum Guides for Parents and the Community at Large

After selecting or developing lifelong learning–centered courses and units, it is beneficial to develop special *curriculum guides* that provide parents and the community at large an overview of key information about the core curriculum by grade level and subject area. These curriculum guides, periodically updated, provide parents and community members with handy, easy-to-understand information on what students will study and learn. They often suggest activities that parents can do at home with their children. They can also be especially helpful to parents and teachers who are new to a school or district.

If schools or districts haven't developed these guides, teachers may want to develop a one- or two-page overview explaining their teaching philosophy, expectations for students, essential questions that students will explore, student learning outcomes during the year or course, and activities for parents to do with their children at home. Many examples of curriculum guides for parents (and teachers) are online. For sample curriculum guides for parents, visit https://bit.ly/39aqGb9, which is the Washington, D.C., public schools website. The Horizon Elementary School (https://bit.ly/2JIaepM), in Sun Prairie, Wisconsin, has excellent parent curriculum guides on their website. Visit **go.SolutionTree .com/21stcenturyskills** for live links to the websites mentioned in this book.

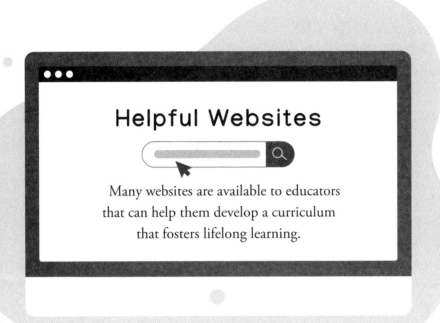

Helpful Websites

Many websites are available to educators that can help them develop a curriculum that fosters lifelong learning.

- Activate Learning at **http://activatelearning.com**

- Curriculum21 at **www.curriculum21.com**

- "Curriculum Mapping" (Jacobs, 2010a) at **www.curriculum21 .com/z-docs/CMpresentation.pdf**

- Massachusetts Department of Elementary and Secondary Education: Model Curriculum Units at **www.doe.mass.edu /frameworks/mcu**

- Project Zero at **https://pz.harvard.edu/projects/teaching -for-understanding**

- "What Is a Curriculum Map . . . and How Do You Make One?" (Zook, 2018) at **https://bit.ly/355wQYB**

Visit **go.SolutionTree.com/21stcenturyskills**
for live links to these and other resources.

Reflections—Chapter 4

The following questions and activities should provoke and stimulate thought and discussion about lifelong learning curriculum.

- Review the descriptions of the twelve criteria (page 106) and consider how you can group the criteria into high, medium, and low priorities. What are your reasons for these priorities? How might this exercise help you use the criteria to analyze the current curriculum or select new curricula?

- Brainstorm the challenges that might exist in attempting to implement a lifelong learning curriculum, either by changing the existing curriculum, adopting new curricula, or designing the curriculum using UbD. How might you overcome one or more of these challenges?

Action Steps—Chapter 4

Consider taking the following action steps to improve the curriculum.

- Use the reproducible "Curriculum Rating System" (page 123) to analyze a classroom or school curriculum. On which criteria would the curriculum rate highly? Which aspects of the criteria could be improved? List recommendations that would improve the curriculum.

- Begin mapping a curriculum currently in place in a classroom or school. Develop a chart with a timeline across the top and rows divided into goals, instruction, assessments, and materials and resources. As you map, consider how well the curriculum meets the twelve criteria and what might improve it.

- Review the UbD template with descriptors and UbD sample units in the following reproducibles: "Citizenship Unit for Elementary Students," "Science Unit for Middle School Students," and "Poetry Unit for High School Students" (page 125). Download the blank UbD template 2.0 (Wiggins & McTighe, n.d.) from https://tinyurl.com/y5wo38mz and use it to design one or more units or courses with it.

Curriculum Rating System

Use this curriculum rating system to evaluate a curriculum currently in use or a curriculum being considered for adoption.

1. Begin by using criteria you think are most important to rate the curriculum, and do a quick evaluation using the 1 to 4 rating numbers.

   1 = Few or no criteria are in the curriculum.

   2 = Some criteria are in the curriculum.

   3 = Many criteria are in the curriculum.

   4 = For the most part, the criteria are included in the curriculum.

2. Add comments for each characteristic to describe your score in greater detail.

3. Decide which criteria to improve first. For example, if the goals of the curriculum are many and listed in terms of behavioral objectives (and you therefore gave a low rating), how can you convert the objectives into a few key understandings and essential questions? If instruction does not meet the characteristics of the four phases, and you gave it a low rating, how can you adapt instruction to incorporate them?

4. If you have time, describe why you assigned the rating number to each criterion. After rating, use the evaluation to determine where to begin improving an existing curriculum or to determine whether to adopt a new curriculum.

page 1 of 2

Criteria	Rating
Is the curriculum focused around a limited core of understandings, big ideas, and essential questions?	
Does the curriculum actively engage students and develop student curiosity and interest in learning?	
Does the curriculum integrate the learning and practice of key lifelong learning skills?	
Is instruction organized to support lifelong learning education goals?	
Does the curriculum include varied and valid assessments?	
Does the curriculum provide opportunities to build on previous learning, learn from helpful feedback, and grow learning over time?	
Does the curriculum promote coherence and learning progressions?	
Does the curriculum include many different types of materials and resources, including technology?	
Does the curriculum take into account students' diverse abilities, interests, and needs?	
Does the curriculum encourage interdisciplinary connections?	
How does the curriculum build in outside and authentic learning experiences?	
Is the curriculum well organized and easy to use?	

page 2 of 2

Citizenship Unit for Elementary School Students

Stage One: Desired Results		
Established Goals	Transfer	
"Fundamental ideas that are the foundation of American constitutional democracy . . . are . . . the rule of law, separation of powers, checks and balances, minority rights, and the separation of church and state." (p. 47)	*Students will be able to independently use their learning to:* Become more active citizens in a democratic society	
	Meaning	
	Understandings	**Essential Questions**
"Rules and laws can serve to support order and protect individual rights." (p. 47)	*Students will understand that:*	• What does it mean to be a good citizen?
"Governments meet the needs and wants of citizens." (p. 47)	• Legitimately developed rules are a key element in creating a democratic society	• Why is it necessary to have rules? What would it be like if we didn't have rules in school?
"Key practices in a democratic society include civic participation based on studying community issues, planning, decision-making, voting, and cooperating to promote civic ideals." (p. 63)	• Active citizenship means helping others and participating in the political process	
	Acquisition	
	Students will know:	*Students will be skilled at:*
	• Citizenship	• Writing a book
	• Good citizenship	• Using discussion strategies
	• Representation and voting	• Developing concepts
	• Bill of Rights	• Developing questions
	• Local government	
	• Federal government	
	• Active citizenship	

page 1 of 4

Stage Two: Evidence	
Evaluative Criteria	**Assessment Evidence**
The following criteria will be used to create a rubric: • Organization and coherence • Key idea comprehension	Performance Tasks: • Create a daily active citizenship chart, illustrating how each day a student is a good citizen. • Create a booklet titled *What Does It Mean to Be a Good Citizen?*
The following criteria will be used to create a rubric for feedback to students on the open-ended assignment: • Factual correctness	Other Evidence: Assessment at the end of the unit. Students explain what they have learned as a result of the unit and share answers with each other.

Stage Three: Learning Plan
Summary of key learning events and instruction, including diagnostic and formative assessments

Setting the Stage
• The teacher introduces the essential questions: What would it be like if we didn't have rules in school? Why is it necessary to have rules? Students, together with the teacher, discuss these two questions and make a list of the reasons we have rules and what would happen if we didn't have them. • The teacher introduces the essential question: What does it mean to be a good citizen? Students discuss and brainstorm answers. The teacher records answers on chart paper and posts them around the room for review and revision at the end of the unit.

Building the Foundation
• The teacher introduces the idea of government and how government helps set the rules for us. Students learn the names and functions of a mayor, governor, and president to help them understand who heads different governments and what the governments and people in those roles do. • Students discuss the idea that they are able to be active citizens and have a voice in how things are run and in making up the rules. They also think about their current roles as citizens (for example, when they helped make up the rules for the classroom). The teacher reads *D Is for Democracy: A Citizen's Alphabet* (Grodin, 2004) and discusses key concepts with students.

page 2 of 4

Building the Foundation

- Students discuss classroom and school rules, why they were developed, and how they might improve them. They work in groups to make suggestions as to how to improve these rules. The class together decides on a list of classroom rules that will be posted around the room for the remainder of the school year. They plan to visit with the principal and share their views on how to improve school rules.

- Students, together with the teacher, examine some fundamental ideas about democratic government, such as representation, voting, and the Bill of Rights. The teacher explains how we elect leaders at all levels by voting for them, how our rights are protected, how our leaders pass laws, and how many people are active in working to elect people who support what they think the laws should be.

- The teacher reads and discusses *The First Book of Local Government* (Eichner & Bacon, 1964). A local councilperson comes to class to explain how the local government works. Together, the class and councilperson create a diagram of how local government works and passes laws. Students ask the questions they prepared in advance. She also reads to students *How the U.S. Government Works . . . and How It All Comes Together to Make a Nation* (Sobel, 2012) and puts key words on the board that explain the federal government system and the purposes it is designed to serve.

- Students discuss the idea of what a citizen is and then brainstorm the characteristics of a good citizen. The teacher reads *I Am a Good Citizen* (Salzmann, 2003) to students. The class begins to think about what they can do on a daily basis to demonstrate good citizenship.

Deepening Learning

- Each student is provided with a daily active citizenship chart where they check off the things they do each day to be a good citizen (for example, following a classroom or school rule, helping a friend, or helping at school and at home, and then listing a problem they helped solve).

- The class goes on a field trip to local government offices, where they meet the mayor and local councilpeople and are taken to their offices to ask them students' questions about how they got elected, what they do during the day, how they help people, and so on.

- Students meet with the school principal to discuss school rules and make suggestions how to improve them. The principal has agreed in advance to consider their suggestions and make changes if appropriate.

page 3 of 4

Providing Closure
• Students share their active citizenship charts and reflect on what they learned by completing them. • Students answer a set of questions to determine what they have learned by the end of this unit. Some of the questions include, Why is it important to have government? What rights are protected by our Constitution? How do people get to be government leaders? What do government leaders do that is important? How is government organized? • Each student creates a booklet titled *What Does It Mean to Be a Good Citizen?* They devote a page each to a different way to be a good citizen (for example, work together, help others, don't litter, or help make the rules). The pages include text and drawings illustrating good citizenship. They share the books with each other, with parents and guardians, and with local politicians.

Additional Resources

Lillian's Right to Vote (Winter, 2015)

Being a Good Citizen (Small, 2006)

Source: Template adapted from Wiggins, G., & McTighe, J. (2011). The Understanding by Design guide to creating high-quality units. Alexandria, VA: Association for Supervision and Curriculum Development. Source for standards: National Council for the Social Studies. (2010). National Curriculum Standards for Social Studies: A framework for teaching, learning, and assessment (Rev. ed.). Silver Spring, MD: Author.

Teaching for Lifelong Learning © 2021 Elliott Seif • SolutionTree.com
Visit **go.SolutionTree.com/21stcenturyskills** to download this free reproducible.

Science Unit for Middle School Students

Stage One: Desired Results		
Established Goals	**Transfer**	
• "The student develops a familiarity with the sky."	*Students will be able to independently use their learning to:*	
• "The student knows our place in space."	• Understand the place of the earth in the universe	
• "The student knows the role of the Sun as the star in our solar system."	• Gain perspective regarding place, size, and scale	
	• Understand how scientists infer knowledge from things not directly observed	
• "The student knows the characteristics and life cycle of stars."	**Meaning**	
• "The student knows the scientific theories of cosmology."	**Understandings**	**Essential Questions**
	Students will understand that:	• Who are we?
	• The earth is infinitesimal when compared to the universe	• What is our place in the universe?
	• Scientists must use many different methods to gather data about the universe	
	• Data collected now can help us understand the past and predict the future	
	Acquisition	
	Students will know:	*Students will be skilled at:*
	• The universe is composed of many different kinds of objects, including stars, nebulae, and galaxies	• Visualizing and interpreting data
	• Information about the universe, such as the following.	• Comparing different objects in the universe, stars at different stages of development, and so on
	◇ The earth is one of many planets orbiting our star, the sun.	• Making data-related predictions about future aspects of the universe
	◇ The sun is one of many (100–400 billion) stars in our galaxy, the Milky Way.	• Creating and using different types of visual organizers
	◇ The Milky Way is one of many (over fifty-four) galaxies in our galaxy group, the Local Group.	• Explaining concepts to younger students
	◇ The Local Group is one of many (one-hundred-plus) groups.	

page 1 of 4

Stage Two: Evidence

Evaluative Criteria	Assessment Evidence
The following criteria will be used to create a rubric: • Accuracy of information • Quality narrative • Quality explanations • Creativity	Performance Tasks: Writing a storybook—This assignment tasks each student with becoming a children's book author and guiding their young readers on a journey through the cosmos. The storybook's ultimate goal is to convince younger students to appreciate our place in the universe.
The following criteria will be used to create a rubric for feedback to students on the open-ended assignment: • Accuracy of information • Conceptual understanding	Other Evidence: • Short open-ended essays • Visual organizers • Flowcharts • Quizzes • Exit slips • KWL activity

Stage Three: Learning Plan

Summary of key learning events and instruction, including diagnostic and formative assessments

Setting the Stage

• Introduce the unit by briefly examining and discussing the essential questions, Who are we? What is our place in the universe? Ask students to look up at the sky this evening and think about what they see there, then write brief answers to the questions, and bring in their answers the next day. Collect the answers and revisit them for review and rewrites at the unit's end. Encourage students throughout the unit to look up at the sky and notice what they can about its size, the objects there, and the distance those things are from the earth.

• Students will discuss the question, What can we gain by studying astronomy? Provide some quotes that illustrate why it's important and powerful. Students will brainstorm their ideas about its importance and these will go on newsprint and be posted around the room.

• Show a photo of the earth taken from outer space. Discuss with students what the planet looks like from space, the earth's shape, size, continents, and seas, and what it tells us about its place (and ours) in the universe.

• Students will read, see a slideshow about, and discuss a history of discoveries of the universe, recent spaceship voyages into outer space, and some recent amazing discoveries about the earth and the universe. Students will use a visual organizer worksheet to together create a timeline of events and discoveries.

• Do a KWL activity: What do you know about the universe? What would you like to know? Have students fill out the first two columns of the KWL. They will revisit the KWL at the end of the unit and fill in what they have learned about the universe.

• Introduce the performance task (storybook project). Have students read through the handout, storyboard, and writing prompts. Answer questions and explore the mechanics of the project, due dates, and so on. Stress the idea that this will be a gradual process of developing the project.

Teaching for Lifelong Learning © 2021 Elliott Seif • SolutionTree.com
Visit **go.SolutionTree.com/21stcenturyskills** to download this free reproducible.

Building the Foundation

- Students will read text and watch several videos examining the origins of the universe, its changes, and its inevitable end. We will discuss what they have read and seen, and then each student will create a timeline on the universe's origins and development.

- Take students through a presentation on the star lifecycle so they can create a flowchart on the board for various stellar masses and their fates.

- Use a slide show to help students imagine a voyage from earth into space. Ask students to draw the feelings they had as they moved away from earth far into space. Post the drawings around the room and do a gallery walk, then have a discussion.

- Provide factual information about our planet, moon, sun, stars, and so on. Have students fill out the graphic organizer with information as you share it. Ask students to think about how they can convey the idea of great lengths of time, space, and distance to students through writing and images. *Ask students to fill out a graphic organizer as the information is shared.*

- Have students group and label different types of galaxies. Discuss the types and how students think some were formed or destroyed.

Deepening Learning

- Ask each student to conduct research and find one reading or media presentation about our place in the universe that adds to what has already been learned. Students bring in the reading or media presentation to share with the class.

- Begin the performance task: writing a storybook for elementary or younger middle school students that helps them appreciate and understand the universe and encourages them to learn. Explain that each story must include a description of different kinds of objects in our solar system, stars at each different stage of their life cycle, different types of galaxies, and different levels of organization. Students must show evidence that they understand the size of and distance between each of these objects, our solar system's location in the Milky Way, and the ways scientists visualize deep space objects.

- Work on the storybook, including main character, narrator, and plot, and how they will integrate information about the earth and its place in the universe. They also consider drawings to create.

- If possible, have one or more telescopes available during free time. Let them sign out the telescope for use during the evening hours.

- Students can find out more about the universe and our place in it, and hand in a reflection and report on what they discovered for extra credit.

Providing Closure

- Students complete the storybook. Before the final draft, students can meet in small groups, share their books, and get feedback. When completed, place the books around the room and do a gallery walk. Students will also share their books with students at a local elementary school.

- Students revisit their responses to the essential questions: Who are we? What is our place in the universe? Based on the work they have done, each student will create a reflection and response to these questions through a visual image, poem, or brief written reflection. Post their responses on a bulletin board in the hallway.

- Students return to the KWL they used at the beginning of the unit and, in small groups, complete the last column: what I learned about the universe during this unit. The answers should include anything that individual students learned through their extra work. They share their answers and post them around the room for discussion and reflection.

Teaching for Lifelong Learning © 2021 Elliott Seif • SolutionTree.com
Visit **go.SolutionTree.com/21stcenturyskills** to download this free reproducible.

Providing **Closure**
• Students complete a multiple-choice, short-answer quiz.
• Students will complete a self-reflection and explain what they liked about this unit, what they would change, the major things they earned, and what they might do in the future to continue learning about the universe.

Additional Resources

Source for template: Adapted from Wiggins, G., & McTighe, J. (2011). The Understanding by Design guide to creating high-quality units. Alexandria, VA: Association for Supervision and Curriculum Development. Source for standards: Texas Education Agency. (2009). Chapter 112. Texas Essential Knowledge and Skills for science subchapter C. High school. Accessed at http:// ritter.tea.state.tx.us/rules/tac/chapter112/ch112c.html#112.33 on January 6, 2021. Source for unit: Webber, M. A. (2019). Looking up! What is our place in the universe? An astronomy UbD for 8th grade. Accessed at https://digitalcommons.trinity.edu/educ_understandings/445 on January 5, 2021.

Teaching for Lifelong Learning © 2021 Elliott Seif • SolutionTree.com
Visit **go.SolutionTree.com/21stcenturyskills** to download this free reproducible.

Poetry Unit for High School Students

Stage One: Desired Results	
Established Goals	**Transfer**
"The student develops oral language through listening, speaking, and discussion." "The student uses print or digital resources to determine the meaning, syllabication, pronunciation, word origin, and part of speech." "The student reads grade-level text with fluency and comprehension." "The student analyzes the effect of graphical elements such as punctuation and line length in poems across a variety of poetic forms such as epic, lyric, and humorous poetry."	*Students will be able to independently use their learning to:* • Understand poetry and its different forms • Express thoughts and emotions through written poetry

Meaning	
Understandings	**Essential Questions**
Students will understand that: • Poetry is a very different way of writing than prose • Poetry is a form of expressing thoughts and emotions • There are many forms of poetry, and each has its own set of rules to follow	• What is poetry? • How is writing a poem different from writing prose? • What are the forms and rules of poetry?

Established Goals (continued)	**Acquisition**	
"The student composes literary texts such as personal narratives, fiction, and poetry using genre characteristics and craft."	*Students will know:* • Definitions of poetry • Different forms of poetry and the specific characteristics of each type • That poetry is a form of personal expression	*Students will be skilled at:* • Distinguishing between poetry and prose • Distinguishing between different types of poetry • Extracting meaning from poetry • Writing poetry

Stage Two: Evidence	
Evaluative Criteria	**Assessment Evidence**
The following criteria will be used to create a rubric: • Matches poetry criteria • Well organized • Coherent • Has meaning	Performance Tasks: • Students will create their own poetry using the different formats studied in class. • Students will have the opportunity to take part in a poetry slam and share their poetry with classmates and others. Open-Ended Assignment: • Select an essay of interest and turn it into a poem using one of the studied formats. • Write an analysis of a poem. • Create a visual organizer of a poem.

page 1 of 3

Evaluative Criteria	Assessment Evidence
Knowledge and understanding of poetry exhibited through each of the assessments	Other Evidence: • Exit slips • Assessments of understanding of different types of poetry • Poetry portfolio • Self-reflections

Stage Three: Learning Plan

Summary of key learning events and instruction, including diagnostic and formative assessments

Setting the Stage

- The teacher introduces the unit by discussing why poetry is an important way to communicate, reading several examples of poems by leading poets (such as Robert Frost), and asking what the poems communicate and mean to students. The teacher will explain that this unit explores poetry like those read, how poetry differs from prose, and the different types of poetry. One goal is that students will understand why poetry is such an important part of the communication experience.

- The teacher reads the poem "Fog" (Sandburg, 1916) to the class and asks, "Is this a poem? Why or why not?" The teacher briefly introduces and discusses the meaning and forms of poetry and asks students, "What is a poem? How does it differ from prose and other forms of communication?"

- The teacher reads a variety of writing selections, both poetry and prose. After each selection, the class discusses the following questions: Is this selection a poem? Why or why not? What makes it different from a prose (poetry) selection? If yes, what feelings and thoughts does the poem suggest to you? Do you like this poem? Why or why not?

- Using a concept-attainment exercise, students work in groups with a variety of short selections of both poetry and prose. They decide which selections are poetry and which are not. They then determine the characteristics of the poetry selections. Students should begin to consider such things as meter, rhyme, rhythm, and concise meaning as key aspects of poetry.

- Based on the activities and discussions, together, students write a beginning definition of a poem that they will examine and revise at the end of this unit.

Building the Foundation

- Students further examine different forms of communication and consider when and why they are used. Working in small groups, students fill out a Forms of Communication chart with three columns: What is it? When do we use it? Why do we use it? The different forms of communication might include songs, fictional stories, letters, research papers, news stories, op-ed pieces, and poetry, to name a few.

- During a number of Socratic seminars, the teacher reads a poem to the class and asks for reactions and interpretations. The students discuss the poem's background, form, style, devices, and meaning.

- Students start a poetry portfolio by finding and identifying many examples of different types of poetry to place in their portfolios. They label each poem with its type (limerick, diamante, haiku, blank verse, and so on).

- A poetry slam is conducted in class. Up to ten student volunteers find a poem that they like and read it to the rest of the class. The class reacts to each poem to identify and examine its type, organization, and meaning.

- The teacher introduces and reviews the many types of poetic devices and terminology, including alliteration, hyperbole, metaphor, rhyme, similes, and other devices.

page 2 of 3

Deepening Learning

- Students begin writing a poem based on an essay that is of interest to them. They examine essays online and in a text, and then decide which essay to turn into a poem. Once decided, they will draft a poem based on one of the forms learned earlier, using a variety of devices. They have a choice to draft a poem and share it with their teacher and others before it is completed.

- Students select a poem from a number provided by the teacher. Using the poem and any research conducted about the poem and its background, they will write a reflective and analytical essay about the poem's form and meaning.

Providing Closure

- Students reexamine their initial definition of a poem (from the setting the stage phase), reflect on the definition, and make changes based on the work they did for this unit.

- Each student creates a visual image of poetry using the definition and other work from this unit. These visual images will be posted around the room and shared in a gallery walk.

- Students have the opportunity to take part in a poetry slam and share their poetry with classmates and others. The audience will have a chance to briefly discuss each poem and reflect on its meaning.

- The teacher selects several from among those poems written by students to enter into a poetry competition.

- Students will write a self-reflection on this unit, discussing what they learned, what went well, what was exciting, what was surprising, and what they will carry forward as a result of this unit.

- Students add to their poetry portfolio the final definition of poetry and their visual image, their self-reflection, their own poetry, their written reflection and analysis of their chosen poem, completed worksheets on poetic forms and poetic devices, and the examples of different types of poetry selected earlier. They submit the portfolio to the teacher for review and evaluation.

Additional Resources

- Poetry Foundation at www.poetryfoundation.org

- Poets.org at https://poets.org/poetry-teens

- Haiku Poem Interactive at www.readwritethink.org/files/resources/interactives/haiku

Source for template: Adapted from Wiggins, G., & McTighe, J. (2011). The Understanding by Design guide to creating high-quality units. *Alexandria, VA: Association for Supervision and Curriculum Development. Source for standards: Texas Education Agency. (1998).* Chapter 110. Texas Essential Knowledge and Skills for English language arts and reading subchapter B. Middle school. *Accessed at http://ritter.tea.state.tx.us/rules/tac/chapter110/ch110b.html#110.24 on January 5, 2021. Source for unit: Dougherty, K. (2008).* I didn't know that was poetry [8th grade]. *Accessed at https://digitalcommons.trinity.edu/educ_understandings/60 on November 18, 2020.*

Teaching for Lifelong Learning © 2021 Elliott Seif • SolutionTree.com
Visit **go.SolutionTree.com/21stcenturyskills** to download this free reproducible.

CHAPTER 5

Including Project-Based Learning and Civics Education

Today, when we refer to a school as "high achieving"
those words refer ... [primarily] ... to one thing: good test
scores on basic skills. . . . There is no mention of whether
students are work-ready and life-ready or have the skills
and dispositions to be respectful and active citizens.

—Ron Berger, Libby Woodfin,
and Anne Vilen

In this chapter I will examine two additional components of a strong lifelong education program: (1) project-based learning (PBL) and (2) civics education. PBL has the potential for creating exciting, inviting, and challenging instruction that strongly supports the development of lifelong learning goals. PBL involves students in a variety of interesting projects at any grade level, some through subject-area units of study, some through interdisciplinary projects and units of study, and some through the creation of student-centered projects. Authentic, real-world projects help students learn about careers, current issues and events, significant problems, community service, and active citizenship.

Second, civics education is an important component of a strong lifelong learning education. Active, thoughtful citizenship is a critical educational goal in a world where issues become more complex and young people less involved in the political process (United Nations Educational, Scientific and Cultural Organization, n.d.;

Winthrop, 2020). Yet, while the current standards movement often tends to promote the broad goal of citizenship, state standards are often unfocused with respect to citizenship education.

Project-Based Learning

Lillian G. Katz, Sylvia C. Chard, and Yvonne Kogan (2014), in their book *Engaging Children's Minds: The Project Approach*, explain that projects are:

> an extended in-depth investigation of a particular topic . . . of interest and particular value to students. The investigation includes a wide variety of research processes and procedures that involve children in seeking answers to questions they have formulated individually as well as together in cooperation with the teacher. (p. 3)

Projects often culminate in a product (such as a poster, research paper, persuasive essay, or formal presentation) that students share with the teacher and often with others, including peers, parents and guardians, and the community at large.

Ideally, PBL engages students in a variety of interesting projects that helps them understand lifelong knowledge and skills and develop a growth mindset (Larmer, Mergendoller, & Boss, 2015; Markham, 2012). Some projects are focused around specific subject areas, such as famous inventors or an animal facing extinction. Science projects can help students learn fundamental science concepts and important scientific and mathematical processes, including how to develop and test hypotheses, set up experiments, and explain and predict results. Civics projects enable students to examine, evaluate, and develop positions on and solutions to current problems faced by citizens. Some projects might be interdisciplinary, such as a project on the impact of climate change, or a scientific discovery or technological invention that changed history. Interdisciplinary projects help students see connections between different content areas and enable teachers to work collaboratively. Finally, sometimes students choose what projects they wish to pursue.

Every grade level can incorporate PBL. Even kindergarten students can begin learning project skills and exploring questions independently and in small and large groups (Katz et al., 2014). Also, students can develop projects individually or through group efforts. Both approaches to PBL are important. Individual projects increase personal learning and achievement in many areas, while group projects create many more opportunities for shared learning, the use and development of multiple talents, and collaborative and conflict-resolution skills.

As part of project-based learning, teachers provide students with complex tasks that are often designed to interpret literature and artwork, write stories and plays, draw conclusions from experiments, and write position papers. Textbook teaching, traditional worksheets, short-answer tests, and memorization may be part of project-based learning, but they are only used when they help complete a larger, more meaningful task. The tasks often culminate in a written paper, a book, an oral presentation of a solution to a problem, a work of art, a theatrical performance, a video production, a simulation, or a combination of these. Figure 5.1 illustrates a number of examples of project tasks at all grade levels.

Elementary School	
Elementary school, science	What keeps plants alive? We will grow plants in our classroom. Each student will have a plant to research, including what it needs to survive (for example, water and sunlight). You will take care of your plant, keep a record of what you do to help it thrive and survive, and determine how well it survives in the classroom environment. After a period of time, you will make a short presentation to the class about this information.
Elementary school, social studies	What is a community? You will interview your parents or guardians about the history of the community, learn about who lived in the community in earlier times, visit local businesses and organizations in the community, interview local businesspeople and members of local organizations, and learn about local government. The final product will be a book illustrating what you learned about what makes up a community and ways to improve the community.
Elementary school, interdisciplinary	How are buildings designed and constructed? Learn about building design and construction by learning how our school was built and designed. You will measure the classrooms to learn about the design features and materials used to build the school. We will interview the custodians to find out how they take care of the building, how the heating and cooling systems work, what cleaning materials are used, and other maintenance work. Small groups will design and construct their own building, and then explain the design and its use, size, construction materials, and any other characteristics you would like to share.

Figure 5.1: PBL ideas for all grade levels.   *continued →*

Upper elementary school, social studies	What are the diverse cultures that make up our country? Students will develop scrapbooks that describe their own lives and their family's. They interview family members and write a history, including the foods they eat, the country they came from, the traditions they brought with them, and any languages they speak.
Upper elementary school, English language arts	How do you write a play based on a story? Select a story from your reader to adapt into a play. Working together in a group, retell the story using dialogue and agree on the part each person in the group shall play. Select one prop to signify each character. After a few days of practice, read the play to the class as a reader's theater production.
Upper elementary school, interdisciplinary	What is happening to our earth? Is climate change a real problem? What can we do about it? Your job is to do research on climate change and its effects on the earth, and create a short public service announcement (PSA) that will help everyone understand the problems of climate change and what they can do about it. Once you have some ideas, you will work with a small group of students to develop the points that you want to make and create a story board that will help you develop the PSA.
Middle School	
English language arts	How does a book relate to its author's personality and experiences? After reading a book, you will research the author and determine what in the book reflects the author's experiences. You then put together a poster with words, phrases, artwork, photos, and other items that illustrate the connection between the author's life experiences and the essential features of the characters in the book.
Life skills	What career are you interested in? What's your plan to prepare for this career? Create an exhibition that illustrates information about a specific career or career area that interests you and what it takes to pursue that career. Use information from interviews, books and articles, photos and slides, videos, software, and other media. Your exhibition will be part of a career fair that will enable you to share your information with other students.
Mathematics	What is a living wage? Examine how much different types of households need in order to cover expenses such as food, housing, transportation, and medical care. Compare your findings with average wages and minimum wages in our area. Recommend a minimum wage and how much families should earn in order to be able to pay their expenses.

Science	Can humans survive by eating only invertebrates? Conduct research to find out more about invertebrates. Go to the supermarket to find a variety of invertebrates. Classify the invertebrates that you find. Determine if someone could obtain a balanced diet on a meal of nothing but invertebrates. Be prepared to share your results with the rest of the class.
Social studies	What is life like for Inuit? How does it compare with our lives? Small groups select one of the following topics on Inuit and their environment: Inuit transportation, homes, food, family life, or a topic of your choice approved by the teacher. Use a variety of sources (for example, texts, photos of Inuit life, and audiovisual materials) to locate and record all information necessary to complete the project. Groups will compare what they learn about the aspect of Inuit life that they study with their own lives. Finally, your group will decide the best way to present the information (for example, a PowerPoint presentation or a collage) and create a presentation to share with the class.

High School

Civics	How can I be of service to others? Find a local community organization to volunteer with, conduct research about the organization, and document thirty hours of volunteering with logs, journals, photos, interviews, newspaper articles, and any other sources. Put together a presentation about the work of the organization and your volunteer work to share with others.
English language arts	Who is a hero? How do people become heroes? Read a book in which there is a hero, heroine, or several heroes or heroines. Write an essay analyzing the nature of heroism through the lens of the book and its heroes. We will share essays and then select five to ten essays that will become part of a collection to share with other students, parents, guardians, and the community at large.
History	What's your viewpoint? How do you support and justify it? Consider the information your teacher provides explaining both sides of an issue that has societal impact, such as Medicare for all. Research the issue's history and choose which side of the issue you support. Prepare and deliver a presentation, using any format (oral, written, or video) that presents the arguments and evidence for one side of an issue, and forecasts the consequences of a particular position on society.

continued →

Mathematics	How does mathematics help businesses improve what they do? You are a member of a company task force that has been asked to create a container that can hold the largest amount of material possible. Start by attempting to design and construct the largest possible container from a single sheet of 9 by 12-inch stiff colored paper. When you are finished, determine how large the capacity of the container is. Justify your answer in a report, detailing your activities and sources. All mathematical formulas used must be clearly stated. Keep a log of your progress. We will together examine the results and determine which container has the greatest capacity and why.
Science	How do physical conditions affect the growth and survivability of an organism? Design and carry out an experiment to determine the optimal salinity for brine shrimp survival. Be prepared to share how you developed and conducted your experiment and its results.

These examples illustrate how projects at all grades can help students explore an interesting theme or research an interesting question in English, science, social studies, or mathematics. Some projects help integrate learning from many subjects. Teachers can incorporate projects into a unit or use them as a unit's culminating activity to apply knowledge and skills learned during the unit, or extend their learning through further research. Sometimes a project *is* the unit, as when a teacher begins a unit with questions or problems, asks students to collect, organize, and evaluate information about a topic under study, and then ends the unit by requiring a product or presentation that synthesizes and draws together the entire unit experience. Sometimes projects tie together yearlong experiences in a subject area, and sometimes projects tie together information from a variety of subject areas, such as when an interdisciplinary research unit is developed at the end of the year in an elementary school classroom to enable students to apply their research skills and learn more about a topic studied during the year that interests them.

Many types of products, experiences, and performances enable students to demonstrate the results of their projects. Written documents are very common, such as letters, diaries, logs and journals, essays, stories, poems, plays, and position papers. Graphs and charts are sometimes used as end products to help students organize data. Students, especially in elementary school, often create artwork and crafts that synthesize learning; murals, illustrations, models, and posters are typical examples. Other examples of end products and experiences include the creation of games, stories, poems, theater productions, a video, a television program, or an invention design.

The development of oral, along with visual, presentations gives students a chance to share the results of their work with others and to practice public speaking. Sometimes teachers use a simulation or role-playing scenario to help students understand historical events (for example, by asking students to reenact the Constitutional Convention or the Yalta Conference) or to act out and understand critical events in a novel (for example, the life of children in Charles Dickens's [1837–1839, 1992] *Oliver Twist*).

Some of PBL instruction's major characteristics follow.

- Teach key concepts and understandings.

- Support the development of lifelong learning skills.

- Build the project around an essential question or problem statement.

- Emphasize the development of open-ended, creative tasks and products.

- Use complex measures and criteria to support high levels of success.

- Provide opportunities for feedback, progress, and improvement.

- Complete the project individually or in small groups.

- Organize project instruction around the four phases of instruction.

These characteristics align with the approaches that facilitate lifelong learning: goals, instruction, and assessment (Boss & Larmer, 2018; Markham, 2012).

PBL and Lifelong Learning Knowledge Goals and Skills

Projects are built around a set of core understandings and essential questions that drive the learning. For example, in one senior high school project, the focus of student learning is on censorship. The essential, driving question for this unit is, Should censorship play a role in society (Larmer, Ross, & Mergendoller, 2009)?

PBL also supports the development of the skills described in chapter 1 (page 30) and listed here, that help students be better prepared for lifelong learning (Larmer et al., 2009).

- **Understanding skills:** Students find connections and patterns among discrete facts in order to develop meaningful concepts and ideas; students explain a key concept, idea, or theory.

- **Research-inquiry skills:** Students search for, find, evaluate, and process information and define problems and challenges.

- **Thinking skills:** Students think logically and creatively by sorting, comparing, contrasting, explaining, analyzing, synthesizing, interpreting, creating and critiquing arguments, and creatively solving problems.

- **Communication skills:** Students learn how to coherently and thoughtfully write and speak, and listen to others.

- **Collaboration skills:** Students learn how to work together to design projects, solve problems, and conduct research.

- **Application skills:** Students learn how to apply and transfer their learning to new and novel situations.

In PBL, these skills are often integrated together into activities that enable students to practice and learn holistically. In other words, students think about how to solve a challenging problem and develop a plan for solving the problem and completing the project. They are able to collect, organize, comprehend, and evaluate information and ideas, analyze charts, interpret readings, and synthesize data. They often draw conclusions from a variety of information sources, thus deepening their understanding of a subject under study. The application of mathematical processes helps students understand mathematical concepts and their usefulness. Students often share the wealth of information learned from a variety of projects, thus enriching and expanding their learning.

Instruction

Organizing PBL around the four phases of instruction described in chapter 2 (page 41) helps ensure that students incorporate the key elements of a strong project (PBLWorks, 2019a, 2019b) and also provides a structure for implementing projects. During phase one, when setting the stage, the teacher creates and shares interesting essential questions that will drive students' projects. In phase two—when the teacher is helping students build a foundation of lifelong skills—students learn how to and practice conducting research, writing position papers, organizing information, solving challenging problems, and making powerful presentations. Once students build a foundation of key skills, they move into phase three to dig deeper into project resources, build greater understanding, and draft culminating activities on their own, with little help from the teacher. In phase four, as the teacher is providing closure, students can complete individual and group work and share their results to demonstrate that they have mastered processes and content at high levels of achievement. Figure 5.2 illustrates one way to organize project activities into the four phases of instruction.

Phase One—Setting the Stage
• Provide, share, and discuss a challenging problem with essential questions that are open ended and engaging to begin inquiry into the problem. • Assess student understanding, knowledge, and skills related to the project to determine what to teach during phase two. • Engage students in activities that develop initial interest in the problem or question.
Phase Two—Building the Foundation
• Have students find and evaluate useful resources and conduct initial research into the problem or question. If appropriate, teachers can also find useful resources to share with students. • Help students develop an understanding of the issues through concept development and other thinking activities. • Encourage students to ask further questions.
Phase Three—Deepening Learning
• Give students an opportunity to dig deeper into the question or problem on their own, by having them develop their own driving essential questions, conducting further research, developing a student-led discussion, or analyzing new information and data. • Ask questions that require students to engage in higher-order thinking, such as analysis and synthesis. • Ask students to independently or in small groups develop new and better alternatives and solutions for a question or problem they are investigating.
Phase Four—Providing Closure
• Have students create a product or products and share the results in presentations and exhibitions. • Provide opportunities for students to give peers feedback on their work and to receive feedback from teacher and peers. • Give students the opportunity to reflect on the process and results by answering such questions as, What did you learn by doing the project? What were the best parts? What would you change?

Figure 5.2: Project activities organized into the four phases of instruction—Example.

Figure 5.3 (page 146) provides examples of how to organize different types of projects through the four phases of instruction.

Literacy projects are designed primarily to improve reading, writing, and thinking skills. Their primary characteristics focus on before-during-after activities, such as the following.			
Phase One— Setting the Stage	Phase Two—Building the Foundation	Phase Three— Deepening Learning	Phase Four— Providing Closure
• Select, introduce, and read high-quality fiction and nonfiction. • Discuss upcoming reading and introduce essential questions with the whole class. • Provide context for reading.	• Students read individually or as a group (guided reading). • Teach vocabulary, concepts, and background knowledge. • Students take notes and synthesize information and ideas. • The whole class begins discussing essential questions.	• Discussion is deepened with open-ended, interpretive questions. • Students write an analysis or interpretation of a reading based on open-ended, interpretive questions. • Students conduct a debate.	• Students write and self-reflect on both the content and the process. • Students share thoughts and self-reflections. • Students continue reading independently and in small groups as follow-up.
Science projects emphasize the search for empirical truth backed by evidence. Teachers who use this important strategy will focus their instruction around the following aspects.			
Phase One— Setting the Stage	Phase Two—Building the Foundation	Phase Three— Deepening Learning	Phase Four— Providing Closure
• The whole class identifies and discusses initial science questions, problems, and challenges for exploration.	• Students gather information and data, make observations, conduct research, and analyze many information and data sources, including primary and secondary sources, field experiences, surveys, interviews with experts, and experiments. • Students develop hypotheses for further investigation. They begin to create experiments with teacher support.	• Students conduct further research, and collect, analyze, and further process information and data. • Students test hypotheses by setting up and performing experiments.	• Students draw conclusions, synthesize, and self-reflect. • The whole class shares results.

Authentic tasks and projects are designed to apply learning to real-world issues and problems.			
Phase One—Setting the Stage	**Phase Two—Building the Foundation**	**Phase Three—Deepening Learning**	**Phase Four—Providing Closure**
• Students are presented with an authentic issue or problem. • The teacher introduces and students explore driving questions, enduring understandings, and big ideas, products, and performances. • The teacher assesses background knowledge and skills.	• The teacher provides students with background knowledge, understandings, and key skills. • The teacher introduces students to initial authentic experiences that foster real-life understanding. • Students further explore driving essential questions, conduct research, and develop foundational understanding. • The teacher prepares students for completing performance tasks and other assessments.	• The teacher uses a real-world task or simulation to deepen understanding (for example, designing an amusement park ride). • Students develop deeper understanding through explanation, analysis, interpretation, discussions, and other activities. • Students begin to complete the authentic performance task by creating a real-life solution.	• Students complete performance tasks as key culminating assessments. • Students share presentations in real-life settings and exhibit student work. • Students follow up with implementation strategies. • Students write self-reflections on their work.

Creative problem-solving projects are another approach to teaching and learning, focused around the goals of increasing creativity and creative thinking (Isaksen, Dorval, & Treffinger, 1994; Karpova, Marcketti, & Barker, 2011).			
Phase One—Setting the Stage	**Phase Two—Building the Foundation**	**Phase Three—Deepening Learning**	**Phase Four—Providing Closure**
• The teacher begins with an open-ended problem or question that the class shares and explores.	• Students research the problem. What is this problem about? What information and ideas will help us to understand the problem? • Students determine the "real" problem that will focus attention on the basic underlying problem.	• Students continue their research to uncover more knowledge and understanding, then refine information and ideas to help solve the problem. • Students brainstorm alternative solutions to the problem.	• Students rate and rank alternatives and develop the best solutions. • Students make the solutions workable by developing a plan or several plans for implementation. • Students develop a prototype of the solution plans. • Students share their solutions and plans among themselves or in a real-world setting.

Figure 5.3: Ways to organize projects through the four phases—Example.

PBL and Assessment

PBL uses complex assessment measures, many of which are discussed in chapter 3 (page 81). Evaluating projects includes many different aspects of learning, such as the quality of a student's research, the abilities and skills of the student in completing the project, the student's ability to organize the project work, the quality of the end products and presentations, the student's originality and creativity, and the student's ability to self-reflect on the project process and results. The evaluation process includes many assessment opportunities used to both measure success and achievement and provide feedback to students for them to improve their projects (Fraser, 2018).

Because of their complexity, good projects are not easily evaluated and graded. Rubrics, or rating systems that measure how well students perform on a number of different criteria, can ease the task of evaluating complex projects. (See chapter 3 for an overview of rubric development and use.) Usually the criteria in a rubric are placed on a continuum designed to measure the varied levels of student proficiency or achievement. Figure 5.4 is an example of a rubric developed by a school district in Bucks County, Philadelphia, Pennsylvania, designed to determine student levels of achievement for a senior research project.

Projects also provide many opportunities for formative assessments, an important component of lifelong learning (page 83). Students have many opportunities to share drafts of their work with both teachers and other students, receive feedback, and make revisions. Students also receive informal help as they work on projects.

Each discussion of student work reveals a student's level of understanding, both of knowledge and process. Students are able to take greater pride in their work and are rewarded for their improvement efforts. Teachers help students see connections between long-term efforts and results, important for creating a growth mindset (Dweck, 2006). Teachers can assess students' improvement in understanding and use of project skills and abilities over time through the development of a series of projects at many grade levels and many school levels. As pointed out, teachers can use transition projects at the end of the elementary, upper elementary, and middle or junior high school years to evaluate student understanding and project abilities, and also provide schoolwide opportunities for practicing and improving project-based skills. As also pointed out in chapter 3, teachers can use portfolios to showcase projects and growth over time.

5—Excellent	4—Very Good	3—Acceptable or Satisfactory	2—Not Yet Satisfactory	1—Unacceptable
The project goes beyond stated requirements, showing evidence of originality and creative thinking.	The project meets all stated requirements with high-quality work.	The project minimally meets all requirements.	The project meets some but not all requirements.	The project does not meet requirements.
Research is very thorough and uses numerous, varied resources.	Research is thorough and uses several resources.	Research is accurate but lacks detail and explanation.	Research is scant and lacks detail.	Research, if any, is very limited.
Organization is very well thought out. Presentation is in a clear, logical sequence.	Organization shows planning and is in logical sequence.	There is basic organization, but reasoning is not always clear or logical.	Final product is poorly organized and is difficult to understand.	Final project is very poorly organized and difficult to understand.
Project reflects mastery of language, which is varied, meaningful, and mechanically correct.	Use of language is mechanically correct and competent.	The structure and mechanics are generally correct with some errors.	Written materials have many errors in sentence structure and mechanics.	Materials are poorly written and need considerable work.
Project demonstrates or deals with data and information in an insightful and analytical manner.	Data and information are descriptive and reflect analytical thinking.	Project demonstrates an adequate understanding of data gathered and materials used.	Project does not demonstrate an adequate understanding of data gathered or materials used.	Project indicates poor understanding of concepts, data gathered, and material used.

Source: © Palisades School District, Bucks County, PA. Used with permission.

Figure 5.4: Project-based learning rubric example.

Civics Education

Most students are not adequately prepared in classrooms and schools to take on their roles as citizens. They lack both knowledge required for citizenship and an understanding of civic action. For example, only one quarter of high school students was deemed proficient in civics on recent national assessment results (Orenstein, 2019). How can teachers support the implementation of a strong civics education? The bottom line is that "none of this is easy. Civics education crosses content areas. It has implications for the day-to-day operation of schools. Yet civics remains somewhat marginalized among the content areas" (Sawchuk, 2019). Here are three possible ways to improve civics education in schools and classrooms.

1.   Develop classroom current events programs.

2.   Rethink instruction and assessment.

3.   Create a strong civics curriculum.

Develop a Classroom Current Events Program

Students who participate in current issue discussions have a greater knowledge of and interest in politics, improve their critical thinking and communications skills, and have more interest in civic participation. They also are more likely to say that they will vote and volunteer as adults (Gould, n.d.).

You can provide opportunities to understand and discuss current issues in two ways.

1.   Regularly examine current events at all levels.

2.   Integrate current events into courses and programs.

Regularly Examine Current Events at All Levels

Understanding current event issues and problems at every grade level helps students think critically (Wolpert-Gawron, 2017). Beginning in elementary school, age-appropriate current events can be a regular part of the curriculum, introducing a wide range of current issues through multiple resources, such as special civics materials, newspapers, magazines, and other media. Children's literature raises questions about current issues. Classroom visitors, such as legislators and members of nonprofit organizations, can visit classrooms to answer questions, discuss their jobs, and relate how they help to solve problems. At Newsela (https://newsela.com), you can sort stories by grade level.

At the secondary level, contemporary issues can become a more formal, regular part of the school program. For example, when I taught social studies in a middle school, I required my students to bring in a newspaper article related to a critical issue or problem every Friday and to write a short commentary about it. I shared the articles and commentaries, which led to some fascinating discussions. Sometimes we tracked certain issues, and then they had to find an article related to them. Additional ways to involve students include writing editorials and letters to the editor, investigating and writing news stories, holding debates, and interviewing other students (Gonchar, 2014).

Integrate Current Events Into Courses and Programs

Students can better understand current events and think critically about them when course and unit essential questions apply to current issues and challenges. For example, two essential questions that are catalysts for the study of the Great Depression—What is the appropriate balance of power between government and its citizens? What should the federal government's role be in the lives of its citizens?— might also be used to raise issues about several current issues, such as the debate over Medicare for all and economic inequality.

Current issue exploration should not be limited to social studies, but incorporated into many subject areas. Climate change issues can be examined in science courses. Privacy issues can be raised during a discussion of how to use new technologies. Health issues and bioengineering research issues can be examined in both science and health education. The reliability of data and data bias can be examined as students study mathematics, science, and social studies.

One interesting available resource for teaching civics education is the Digital Civics Toolkit (www.digitalcivicstoolkit.org), an online set of modules developed by the MacArthur Research Network on Youth and Participatory Politics (2018). This resource contains five modules.

1. **Participate in a connected world:** This module enables young people to learn more about face-to-face and online communities and to identify civic issues that are relevant, even urgent, to people in their local communities and in the wider world.

2. **Investigate:** This module focuses on how to understand and judge the credibility of online information.

3. **Dialogue:** This module helps young people understand the features of good dialogue, and to navigate digital and social media in order to find good dialogue about civic issues.

4. **Voice:** This module engages students in learning how they can create, remix, and otherwise repurpose content to share with others in online spaces.

5. **Action:** This module invites students to carefully consider a broad range of possible tactics and strategies they can use in order to respond to issues they care about.

Rethink Instruction and Assessment

The use of the four phases of instruction and engaging instructional strategies can help to develop curiosity about civic issues and enhance the development of a foundation of student understanding of civic issues and related skills. Beginning instruction by raising interesting civics questions and creating a context for civics learning is a critical starting point for good citizenship education. Many of the activities in chapter 2 (page 51), including sequencing, patterning, and visual organizers, help students learn how to organize civic knowledge and ideas. Learning the vocabulary and concepts of civics, conducting civics-related research projects, holding discussions and debates, writing persuasive essays, and conducting simulations that ask students to rewrite foundational documents to adapt to current times (Adler, 2011)—all of these activities promote curiosity and interest in civics learning, help students develop foundational civics knowledge, understanding, and skills, and deepen civics learning.

Reframing assessments to include more civics education performance tasks and projects, persuasive essays, visual learning tools, self-reflections, and open-ended writing assignments, discussions, and debates help ensure a more rigorous civics education.

Create a Strong Civics Curriculum

A high-quality civics education program includes a core curriculum of essential questions and understandings that guide the development of a school curriculum. For example, the following citizenship-based essential questions, derived from the National Council for the Social Studies' (2010) National Curriculum Standards for Social Studies focus civics education around the standards' ten themes.

- What does it mean to be an informed and active citizen in a democratic society?

- What are each citizen's rights and responsibilities in a democratic society?

- How do citizens effect change in a democratic society? In what ways can one person make a difference?

- What are the current critical issues, problems, and challenges facing the United States? The world? How might they be resolved?

- Who are the heroes that helped to develop, preserve, and enlarge democracy? What did they do?

- How have the definitions of democracy and democratic traditions changed over time?

- What is now and what has been the struggle to develop, maintain, and enlarge freedom and democracy?

- Whom should we believe? Why?

- When can conflict be resolved peacefully? When does conflict lead to violence?

- What "culture" and "values" support democracy?

- Should Americans also be "citizens of the world"?

- What is the appropriate balance of power between government and its citizens? Between different levels of government?

- How should government balance individual rights and the "general welfare" for the common good?

- Are Americans fairly represented in their government? Why or why not?

- When is war justified? Which American wars were justified? Which were not?

- Does the Constitution adequately protect American freedoms? Should it be changed?

What about facts? This curricular approach does not denigrate the learning of facts but suggests that factual learning occur in a framework of important ideas, themes, and questions that represent key citizenship issues. Placing facts into a context helps students make connections and understand their relevance. For example, learning factual information about the Constitution and its creation might be easier to accomplish when the following essential questions (National Council for the Social Studies, 2010) are the basis for study: Does the Constitution adequately protect American freedoms? Should it be changed?

Another civics education goal is for students to learn and practice the lifelong education skills and habits of mind that foster civic understanding and practice.

Learning how to find multiple sources and evaluate information for reliability is a critical citizenship skill. Forming patterns, developing explanations, and sorting and organizing information are also critical. There should be many opportunities for students to think in complex ways and make well-informed decisions. The importance of collaborating with others is a major focus as well, so students can learn to be open-minded to other points of view, develop clear, cogent arguments that create individual points of view, and know how to dialogue in a civil manner. Students need to learn how to share and discuss their ideas and arguments in a coherent, logical way.

Finally, *media literacy*—an understanding of propaganda, bias, and diverse perspectives—is critical (Huguet, Kavanagh, Baker, & Blumenthal, 2019). Teachers can integrate media literacy throughout social studies, English language arts, and science courses. Helpful websites for integrating media literacy into the curriculum include the Stanford History Education Group (https://sheg.stanford.edu), which has developed history lessons and assessments that promote civic reasoning, and the News Literacy Project (http://newslit.org), which provides programs and resources for educators to teach students how to be smart, active news and information consumers.

Helpful Websites

Many websites are available to educators who wish to learn more about PBL and civics education.

- Annenberg Classroom: The Annenberg Guide to the United States Constitution at **www.annenbergclassroom.org /constitution**

- Center for Civic Education at **www.civiced.org**

- Digital Civics Toolkit at **www.digitalcivicstoolkit.org**

- High Tech High at **www.hightechhigh.org/student-work /student-projects**

- iCivics at **www.icivics.org**

- PBLWorks at **www.pblworks.org/?ACT=37&id=Fq07H35NRd**

- The Project Approach at **http://projectapproach.org**

Visit **go.SolutionTree.com/21stcenturyskills**
for live links to these and other resources.

Reflections—Chapter 5

The following questions and activities should provoke and stimulate thought and discussion about project-based learning (PBL) and civics education.

- Develop a visual organizer that shows the various PBL components, how they fit together, and how they relate to lifelong learning instruction. Once complete, write down your recommendations for integrating PBL into the curriculum. What might be the rewards? What might be the obstacles? How could you overcome the obstacles?

- Compile a list of this chapter's suggestions as to how to create a better and stronger civics education program at any grade level and in any subject. Add any other ideas to the list that you think would be valuable additions. Place a check next to those you view as most important. Place an E next to those that you think are the easiest to implement. Place an H next to those that might be the hardest to implement. What are the implications of this exercise for creating a better and stronger civics education program?

Action Steps—Chapter 5

Consider taking the following action steps to incorporate project-based learning and civics education into the school program.

- Review figure 5.3 (page 146), which provides examples of how to organize different types of projects through the four phases of instruction. Develop a project plan organized around the four phases and one of the exemplary project-based models in figure 5.3.

- Consider the following questions and summarize what you have learned and better understand about civics education.

    ◇ What are the key points or big ideas that you learned from the civics education section?

    ◇ What questions or concerns do you still have?

    ◇ What action plans would you create for improving teaching and learning?

CHAPTER 6

Taking the Next Steps

*If you do not change direction, you may end up
where you are heading.*

—Lao Tzu

How can teachers and schools transition to a greater focus on a lifelong learning education? How do teachers and schools move in this direction? How do they make the principles, ideas, and practices a part of teaching and learning?

First, I will examine the essential features of lifelong learning classrooms. What might they look and feel like? What do teachers do? What about students? Then I will describe four research-based change principles that lay out steps toward providing a lifelong learning education, illustrate the process of putting these principles into practice with two classroom examples, one elementary and one secondary, and, finally, propose a way to plan for lifelong learning implementation using the four-phase instructional framework.

Essential Features of Lifelong Learning Classrooms

In practice, teachers implement the essential features of a lifelong learning education in different ways. For example, in one fourth-grade classroom described by educational researchers Fred M. Newmann, Dana L. Carmichael, and M. Bruce King

(2016), students learned about the human skeletal, muscular, and central nervous systems. The main idea was for students to learn how systems work together to cause movement, and in order to study this, students focused on three essential questions: (1) Why is this body system important?, (2) How does a person take care of this body system?, and (3) What would happen if the body system broke down? Students divided into three groups after the unit was introduced. Each group studied one body system. Three research centers were set up around the room with multiple texts about the human body and its systems, and students learned how to organize their research findings into notes that helped them write a three-paragraph persuasive essay about why the human body system they researched is important. After revising and editing their first draft, students typed the final draft as a Google Document. The teacher gave feedback as comments on the electronic document. The final document was printed and showcased in a human body project. The projects were then distributed to a broad variety of medical locations and exhibited in area nursing homes, fitness centers, chiropractic offices, dentists' offices, hospitals, and doctors' offices.

In this example, essential questions develop student curiosity about and interest in what is being studied, students conduct research and learn writing skills, feedback is given to improve student work, and student work is exhibited in real-world situations. The instructional process mirrors the four phases of instruction, setting the stage through essential questions; building a foundation of understandings and skills; deepening learning through independent study, feedback, and improvement; and providing closure through the completion and sharing of student work.

In another example, Mehta and Fine (2019) describe how the science curriculum at a Midwestern mathematics and science academy was organized around an inquiry approach to teaching and learning. The inquiry approach begins with a tenth-grade course, designed and taught collaboratively by a team of teachers. In this course, students learn to conduct scientific inquiry and produce a research paper that might be submitted to a scientific journal:

> Students begin by learning [and applying] some basic statistics . . . and then are exposed to some of the scientific literature, because . . . many of the students have not seen or read the peer reviewed professional literature, only textbooks. (Mehta & Fine, 2019, p. 340)

Only after students have developed a foundation of knowledge and skills about scientific inquiry and the nature of scientific papers, and brainstormed what they might be interested in researching, do they write a project proposal, conduct an experiment, and write up the results in the form of a scientific paper. Students conclude the project by creating a poster based on their project as a way of sharing their work and conclusions with the class (Mehta & Fine, 2019).

In this example, student learning revolves around a key big idea—scientific inquiry—and the course actively engages them in an authentic task: becoming scientists doing research and writing a scientific paper of journal quality.

Taken together, these two examples illustrate many of the key indicators of lifelong learning education classrooms.

- Students are encouraged to be curious explorers and to be interested and involved in learning through essential questions and engaging activities.

- Instruction focuses on developing understanding rather than learning discrete facts and information.

- Students learn, practice, and apply lifelong learning skills in order to build understanding, conduct research, use study skills, think critically, write, communicate, collaborate, and apply and transfer their learning.

- Teachers use the four phases of instruction to set the stage, build a foundation of understandings and skills, deepen learning through independent and interdependent activities, and have students complete and exhibit their work.

- Many activities consist of authentic, real-world learning experiences.

- Activities and assessments such as performance tasks and projects, open-ended assignments, and self-reflections are integrated into the learning experiences and assessments.

- Formative assessments and specific feedback improve and grow learning.

Steps Toward a Lifelong Learning Education: Change Principles

These examples illustrate some of the diverse ways teachers and schools might put lifelong learning goals into practice. But these examples also raise questions about the process that led to the development of these approaches to teaching and learning. How did these teachers get there? What did they learn to do differently? How do classroom teachers, schools, or districts move in this direction?

To begin to answer these questions, you will examine four key research-based principles to consider when involved in a change process. Jim Collins and Morten T. Hansen (2011), in their book *Great by Choice: Uncertainty, Chaos, and Luck—Why*

Some Thrive Despite Them All, compared seven very successful organizations with seven failed organizations in the same fields, to discover the reasons for their success or failure. Surprisingly, the successful organizations and their leaders were not more creative, visionary, charismatic, ambitious, lucky, risk seeking, heroic, or prone to making big, bold moves; the successful organizations attended to the following change principles (Collins & Hansen, 2011).

- They planned lofty goals and at the same time exerted discipline while implementing them.

- They implemented the goals methodically and gradually.

- They experimented with several ideas before deciding on one to implement.

- They planned ahead and were cautious during implementation.

Plan Lofty Goals and Exert Discipline in Implementing Them

The leaders and workers in highly successful organizations create "something larger and more enduring than themselves" (Collins & Hansen, 2011, p. 31). They develop something to reach for. Translated into educational terms, great leaders, teachers, and organizations have lofty aims—for example, to promote a growth mindset in all students, to raise the level of critical and creative thinking, to build understanding rather than teach discrete knowledge and skills, and to prepare every child for citizenship in a democratic society, to name some possibilities.

However, what distinguishes successful from unsuccessful organizations is not only their lofty goals but their devotion over time to the implementation of what Collins and Hansen (2011) call a specific, methodical, and consistent (SMaC) approach—a set of "durable operating practices that create a replicable and consistent success formula" for implementing the goals in a disciplined fashion (Collins & Hansen, 2011, p. 128). In simple terms, the approach is the plan—the key ingredients that will help organizations reach their goals. Once established and understood, the goals are pursued with consistent intensity and devotion. Changes to the implementation occur only when it is clear that specific parts of the approach do not help lead to the goals.

Work to Get There Methodically and Gradually

Successful organizations pursue their goals and core values with plans that are implemented over the long haul. They work to make sure that their goals and plans for success are primary considerations over a period of time. They make sure that there is a gradual movement toward improvement, knowing that there will be ups and downs during the process of change.

Collins and Hansen (2011) illustrate this gradual, long-term, disciplined approach to success by describing two different attempts to be the first to reach the South Pole. Both Roald Amundsen and Robert Falcon Scott began trekking to the South Pole at about the same time. Amundsen adhered to a regimen of traveling fifteen to twenty miles a day, in both good and bad weather. Even on really good days, his team only went seventeen miles in order to avoid exhaustion, and on bad days, they still tried to travel fifteen to twenty miles unless the weather was extremely bad and made travel impossible. Scott, by contrast, would move his team in fits and starts—he would drive his team as far as they could go on good days, and complain about the weather on bad days. As Collins and Hansen (2011) report, Scott's team encountered six days of gale-force winds on which they did not travel, while Amundsen's team ran into fifteen days of similar weather but traveled on eight of them. As a result, it took Scott a month longer than Amundsen to reach the South Pole!

Sometimes organizations may be forced to move back one step, or to move forward more slowly, but they can resume their gradual march toward the finish line. They also don't rush to get there. They know that an attempted sprint to the finish line may be a recipe for disaster.

Try Several Ideas Before Deciding on One to Implement

Another difference between the organizations that failed and those that succeeded is that failed organizations tended to latch onto new ideas and innovations and immediately attempted to put them into practice, without gaining evidence as to their potential success or considering how to implement them with precision and accuracy (Collins & Hansen, 2011). Successful organizations reduced the risk of implementing new ideas and innovations and made it more likely that those ideas and innovations would succeed.

Unfortunately, educators in reform mode often look for the big win too soon. Instead of trying new ideas, piloting different programs and options, determining which seem successful in a particular setting, implementing a select group over a period of years until they're done right, and sticking with an innovation long enough to make it work, districts and schools often latch on to something new, ask everyone to implement it, expect success in a short period of time, and then move on to the next new thing before the innovation has taken hold and works well.

Plan Ahead and Be Cautious

Imagine that you go to the beach on a beautiful, warm, sunny day. While you are enjoying lying in the sun, here's what you are thinking: What if it gets cold? What if thunderstorms appear on the horizon? How will I handle these possibilities? Am I prepared? Successful organizations think this way. They have what Collins and Hansen (2011) call *productive paranoia*. They are always considering the negative possibilities, risks, and challenges that might occur, even in good times. They tend to keep more dollars in reserve, take fewer risks, prepare for down markets, consider all the negative things that might happen along the way, and take these into account as they attempt to move forward. They avoid moving in a direction that has too many possible negative outcomes and puts too much on the line, unless they are prepared to handle the negative result.

Two Examples of Putting These Principles Into Practice

In reality, putting these change principles into practice requires some thought, effort, and self-discipline. In planning for lifelong learning educational changes, there are many complexities to take into account, ways to begin, and issues to consider. Teachers and schools have varied goals, students, and circumstances. Many forces work against making the changes necessary to create a more lifelong learning program, including required high-stakes tests, teacher, parent, guardian, and student resistance, and the complexity of the changes. By following the four change principles—(1) setting lofty goals, (2) working to get there methodically and gradually, (3) trying out several ideas before selecting those to implement, and (4) planning ahead and being cautious—successful implementation is more likely.

Here are two scenarios, one for an elementary classroom teacher and one for a secondary social studies teacher. As you read these scenarios, think about how these change principles might be helpful in moving a classroom toward a lifelong learning education approach over time.

An Elementary Teacher Fosters Lifelong Learning

Mayberry School District, located near a major city in the Midwest, is a school district with roughly six thousand students. Most education in the district would be called traditional, with a strong emphasis on the use of behavioral objectives and state standards to define learning objectives and a focus on doing well on the state's reading and mathematics standardized tests. (The district does reasonably well on them.) Textbooks are used throughout the grade levels and are a big part of the learning process.

Due to several professional development sessions, Susan, a second-grade teacher with many years of experience in the district, has begun to reconsider how and what she teaches her students. Her first goal is to create a more active classroom that better engages her students and supports a growth mindset. She intends to implement classroom activities that more often arouse curiosity and interest. Simply put, she would like to see many more of her students develop the curiosity to read, become more engaged in learning mathematics, and take an interest in further learning on their own. Also, she wants to introduce projects. She would like to strengthen the social studies and science curriculum, since currently so much time is spent focusing on literacy and numeracy. And, finally, she is interested in implementing the four-phase instructional model.

Her initial plan for the coming year includes the following.

- Adopt, post, and introduce the phrase *Let's find out* (the idea being that she and the students will inquire together and learn the answers to questions) so that a research-based learning model is used more frequently with her students. As a related goal, she wants to give students more opportunities to learn how to look things up and find out answers to questions on their own.

- Use the twelve lifelong learning curriculum criteria to find and pilot a new science program that promotes active learning, core science understandings, and critical lifelong learning skills.

- Find and purchase books that are more interesting to students, enrich core learning in history, and are teachable through the four phases of instruction.

- Have students choose and complete an end-of-year project. They will search for information, write a summary of what they learn, complete a product, and share what they have learned in a small group.

Susan gets approval from her principal, who has also taken part in the professional development sessions, to research and rate elementary science programs over the summer. She spends time reviewing commercial science programs in order to find the one that best meets the twelve lifelong learning curriculum criteria found in chapter 4 (page 106). After comparing several science curriculum programs against the lifelong learning education curriculum criteria, she finds the right fit. The principal agrees to support her choice of this science program for next year, orders the materials, and also agrees to provide time for her to get professional development training during the coming year.

Over the summer, Susan also selects a set of books that might be of greater interest to her students while also supporting her interest in enriching her social studies curriculum. She will use these books to build an academic vocabulary for social studies and a stronger knowledge base about American history and geography, and to encourage research and thinking skills. The books will enable her students to better understand how individuals have had a major influence throughout the nation's history. Her selected books include works about America's founders, great inventors, captains of industry, and individuals who devoted time and energy to human rights issues. Susan chooses some of these books to read to the class, which employs the four-phase instructional model to first build curiosity about the books and use the books to build a foundation of understandings and skills, deepen learning through further research and independent projects, and then give students the opportunity to share their reflections and project results.

At the beginning of the new school year, Susan puts up colorful signs with *Let's find out* and talks with her students about its meaning. Students brainstorm questions about things they want to know more about. Using one of those questions as an example, she models for her students how to look something up on the computer. As the year progresses, Susan schedules three times a week to read one of the books about individuals in history. She begins by introducing an essential question about the book, then discusses the context of the book, defines new vocabulary, and diagnoses what students know about the topic of the book. During the next phase, she reads the book aloud to her students, using the book to develop understandings and build a foundation of knowledge, concepts, and skills. While they are reading the book together, Susan encourages students, through homework assignments, to find out more about the period of time in history and about the person the book discusses, and share their learning with the class.

After her students have read the book, learned new vocabulary, developed new understandings, and practiced lifelong learning skills, Susan also gives her students opportunities for deeper learning through independent and group project options. She works with the school librarian, who teaches her students how to do research and find additional sources. She uses these projects to teach and improve project and problem-solving skills; she hopes that by the end of the year students will be able to work independently and collaboratively with limited help and guidance from her. She also gives students a chance to share their new thoughts and understandings through presentations and self-reflections. Further, she encourages her students to find and bring books to class about individuals in history. Susan also spends three afternoons a week teaching science units, with many hands-on activities, investigations into scientific phenomena, and examination of new science vocabulary and concepts.

At the end of the year, Susan asks her students to select a topic to develop into their own passion projects. The students brainstorm possible topics, and then each student selects a project that is interesting to him or her. Students develop one question they want to explore and then are given time to do research on the topic, finding multimedia items about the topic they can listen to and readings about the topic they can learn from. They use special software to develop a multimedia project, consisting of a digital image and voice narration. The teacher also arranges for an evening with parents to share the results of the work. The principal and librarian also come to class, and the students share their projects with them.

Overall, Susan feels that this was a worthwhile and very satisfying year of teaching, and that she met many of her goals: her students were much more engaged and enthusiastic about learning, had a better understanding of history, science concepts, and investigation skills, and wrapped up the year with a project of interest to them. But it was also a hard year, because there were so many new ways of teaching that she introduced, new things she had to learn, and adjustments to managing her students. In some ways, she felt like a first-year teacher all over again! She hopes for and expects improvements next year, and suspects that these changes will become easier to implement and that next year will be even more satisfying.

A Secondary Teacher Fosters Lifelong Learning

Bob, a high school social studies teacher in a large urban district, is dissatisfied with his teaching. His students don't show much interest in his major social studies course. When he teaches, he follows the district's guidelines: he puts his behavioral objectives on the board, starts his lessons with *do now* activities, and tries to involve his students in his lesson activities. He reads about and discusses lifelong learning education ideas and practices and is intrigued.

The first thing he decides to do, with his principal's OK, is refocus some units around a few interesting, provocative essential questions. He thinks about how he can build his units around questions that relate more to his students' lives and issues of interest, such as their environment, the difficulties many face at home, the challenges they and their families are most likely to be concerned about, issues and questions relevant to their generation's future, and their hopes and dreams for the future. He also realizes that he should gear his units more toward essential questions, understandings, and skills that promote active citizenship.

Here are some of the essential questions Bob comes up with as potential starting points for different units in history.

- Why do people explore? When have you been an explorer? What has it meant to you?

- Why do people decide to come to this country? Where did they come from and how did they get here?

- Is violence ever justified? Why is there so much violence?

- Who has been and is being treated unjustly? Why? What can be done about it today?

- What are the critical features of our government's guiding documents? How would you change them?

- What role does the government play in making our lives better, if any? Where has the government fallen short? Where has it been successful?

- Who were our greatest leaders and why?

- Who were some of our greatest citizens? Why?

- How have civic organizations and individuals improved our lives?

- What are the basic principles of the economic system? Do they promote fairness? How would you change them?

- What does it take to succeed in this country?

- Whom would you vote for?

Bob also decides that he relies too much on the textbook alone for information. The textbook will now become just one of many sources of information in his classroom, and research-based learning ("Let's find out things together") will become a bigger part of his students' learning experience. He begins to collect and post many additional resources that his students can use in class, and he also decides that he will ask his students to search for their own resources for the units they study and share them with the class electronically.

As he progresses through the school year, Bob intends to learn more about and then introduce the interactive notebook to all his history students, so that students can learn how to take notes from readings using the SQ3R strategy and complete more complex, thoughtful activities that extend and apply their learning in another section.

Another change Bob decides to make is that at the end of this year, he will give his students a choice of projects to research and complete. Bob also decides to talk with the English teachers in his school to see if some of their literature readings and writing assignments can be tied more closely with history classes during the coming years. He also hopes that he can coordinate his project activities and writing assignments with how his students are learning to write in their English classes.

At first, Bob's students are confused by the changes, but as they begin to discuss and explore the essential questions he's created, they become more engaged in class activities, develop a greater interest in history, and begin to understand its connection to their lives. Class reading is difficult, but students enjoy reading together in class and figuring out how to learn from the text and other sources of information. Some of the readings students find on their own raise questions during class discussions about how to interpret history and challenge students to think about history in different ways. Homework assignments are based on extending and applying student learning, using the interactive notebook to complete assignments such as graphic organizers so they are interesting for students to complete, share, and discuss. Bob learns from many of his students that they are sharing and talking more with the adults in their lives about what they are learning in class.

Working on a course project is also difficult at first. Bob's students aren't sure how to develop their projects, and he has to learn and share a step-by-step project-development process. But once they select a project that interests them and follow the steps, they enjoy the experience. The first projects are difficult to complete, and the results mediocre, but students are proud of their work and develop some important skills from doing the work.

In the past, Bob's final exam has been very traditional, primarily using multiple-choice questions to review facts, and his students have neither enjoyed taking his exam nor done particularly well on it. This year, he changes his test so that it is more mastery centered, with most questions focused on key information and understandings that have been emphasized in class. He also gives students more time to answer these questions and reviews the test with them. He also adds a final essay exam focused around the question, Which period in history has had the greatest effect on our lives today? This question is open book, and students know the question in advance so they have a chance to pull together information from many sources in response. Bob devotes some class periods prior to the exam so students have a chance to think about how they would answer this essay question, share their thoughts in small groups, and discuss their ideas with the entire class. This year, Bob also gives his students a chance to reflect on what they have learned at the end of each unit and at the end of the course.

All in all, this is a much better year of teaching for Bob than his previous years. He believes his students have learned and retained more than in the past, were much more engaged, and are better prepared to take on their role as citizens.

The Four-Phase Instructional Framework for Planning and Implementing Lifelong Learning

Given the two scenarios and the four change principles previously discussed, how does a teacher or school organization systematically work toward the implementation of a lifelong learning educational approach? One possible approach is to plan for change and conduct professional development using the four phases of instruction described in chapter 2 (page 41). In the two scenarios in this chapter, the first phase of change toward lifelong learning was to set the stage by introducing and initially learning about lifelong learning ideas and adopting goals for change. A second phase was to learn more about lifelong learning and then introduce, pilot, and implement several lifelong learning changes—in other words, to begin building a foundation for lifelong learning. Phase three continues the learning, piloting, and implementing of new ways of teaching and learning that create a tipping point of innovative practices for transforming teaching and learning. Finally, phase-four activities continue to build on, refine, extend, and expand lifelong learning practices. Throughout this process, teachers are sharing ideas and learning from others.

What might happen in each of these professional development planning phases? The following sections provide examples, for each phase, of potential activities and questions for moving toward a lifelong education program. The reproducible "Designing a Lifelong Learning Education Professional Development Plan" (page 180) is a planning tool using the four phases. It summarizes the suggested steps.

Step One: Set the Stage

Consider the following.

Develop an Initial Understanding of What a Lifelong Learning Education Means

Read and discuss this book's introduction, list the changes happening in today's world, and brainstorm initial thoughts on ways to revise current educational goals and practices to help students cope with a changing world.

Based on the inevitability of changes in both world events and learning theories and research, explain why our schools, classrooms, and districts will need to move toward a lifelong learning education program over time. Develop a beginning working definition of lifelong learning education.

Read about the goals of a lifelong learning education in chapter 1 (page 17) and then brainstorm your own set of goals. List the responses from other teachers and sort and classify them into categories. For example, categories could include general goals, instruction, assessment, and curriculum, or you can devise some other system that works to sort and classify the results.

Develop an understanding of key lifelong learning education ideas—goals, instructional approaches, assessments, and curriculum criteria. Divide into groups of four. Each person in each group selects a number from one to four. All the number ones form a group, all twos form a group, and so on. One of the four groups reads chapter 1 on goals, a second reads chapter 2 on instruction, and so on. These groups then discuss the chapters they read and develop a way to summarize and share the main points of each chapter. Once this task is complete, the members rejoin their initial groups, where each member shares the main ideas of the assigned chapter. Once this is complete, the larger group together discusses the key ideas gleaned from this activity and begins identifying a few goals worth pursuing.

Pose and Discuss Initial Essential Questions

Begin reading about and examining the ideas behind a lifelong learning education. Discuss the meaning of lifelong learning. Then pose essential questions to guide initial understanding of what a lifelong learning education includes. Examples of essential questions follow.

- Why lifelong learning? What is happening in the world that suggests students need a more rigorous education?

- What does lifelong learning mean? What are key lifelong learning education goals for students?

- What are the purpose, goals, and outcomes of my (our) current program? What am I (are we) trying to accomplish with our students? Am I (are we) successful? Is it enough?

- Am I (are we) currently preparing my (our) students to live in today's and tomorrow's world? How so or how not?

- Am I (are we) providing students with a lifelong learning educational experience? How can I (we) do better?

- (Elementary) Am I (are we) preparing students with a core understanding of the larger world around them? In science? History and geography? The arts? Literature?

- (Secondary) Am I (are we) engaging students? Teaching too much content? Promoting understanding? Building a foundation of key skills?

- How do I (we) help students learn how to research, searching for information and ideas? Think and reason? Write well?

- Am I (are we) preparing our students to be curious explorers? To be independent, self-directed learners?

- How can I (we) work with others to develop a lifelong learning education rather than each of us doing our own thing?

Create a Lifelong Learning Education Mission and Vision

Use the reproducible "Planning Tool for Creating a Mission and Vision Statement" (page 182) to analyze current practices and make suggested changes to educational goals, instructional practices, assessment practices, and curriculum. Use the results of this analysis to help create and adopt a lifelong learning mission and vision statement. Figure 6.1 provides an example of a mission and vision statement created from responses to this activity.

We envision creating educational experiences for all our students that will do the following.

- Sustain and develop their interest and curiosity in learning.

- Build a broad foundation of concepts and understanding of the world around us and the issues and challenges faced by all.

- Create a foundation of skills and habits of mind that enables all students to do research, read and write well, think critically and creatively, collaborate, present and share their work, apply learning to new and novel situations, and develop a growth mindset.

- Develop their ability to dig deeper into learning and learn independently and interdependently.

- Engage students in the learning process and provide them with feedback that improves their work.

- Broaden and enrich their learning through multiple, meaningful, authentic experiences within and outside of school.

- Redefine the assessment experience and incorporate open-ended assignments, interactive notebooks, performance tasks and projects, self-reflections, and portfolios.

Figure 6.1: Example lifelong learning mission and vision statement.

Explore the Student Outcome Implications of a Lifelong Learning Education

After deciding on a lifelong learning education mission and vision, focus on what student behaviors, knowledge, skills, and habits of mind graduates of your class, course, school, or district should have as a result of this new approach. Make an outcomes list to help you determine what to focus on in the implementation process. Create, for example, a *graduate profile*, which outlines what skills a school believes students should possess when they graduate, and start by asking yourself the following questions.

- What are the key understandings that students should learn as a result of their schooling?

- What cognitive skills and competencies should students do well as a result of their schooling?

- How do students show that they have the desire to continue learning and growing after they graduate?

Analyze Current Lifelong Learning Education Strengths and Obstacles

Once the mission, vision, and outcomes are determined, consider the strengths of the current program and the obstacles that you will face during the implementation process. Which outcomes are currently being realized? Which are not? What obstacles prevent you from implementing your vision and outcomes? Consider not only the classroom obstacles but also school and environmental obstacles, such as parent expectations, state tests and assessments, student resistance, and so on. If possible, contact others who have faced these obstacles and changed their program to a more lifelong learning experience. Use the reproducible "Lifelong Learning Education Analysis" (page 183) for this step.

Teachers who wish to consider teaching with more lifelong learning educational experiences and who have accepted and adopted a mission, vision, and outcomes need to analyze their own teaching. Individually, or in teams, these teachers should answer the following questions.

- What makes it difficult to move in a lifelong learning education direction?

- What am I (are we) doing well? What can be improved?

- Where's a good place to start making changes? What small steps can I (we) take to move in a lifelong learning education direction?

Develop an Initial Implementation Plan

Once these steps and analyses are completed, a teacher, team of teachers, school, or district needs to decide on where to begin the change process. Explore questions such as, What do I (we) need to do to get started?, What steps should I (we) take?, and What are the obstacles, and how can I (we) overcome them?, and use the answers to begin developing an initial plan. You can use the reproducible "Designing a Lifelong Learning Education Professional Development Plan" (page 180) for this step.

Some examples of beginning steps follow.

- Develop a few course units to pilot, built around the UbD template.

- Adopt the four-phase instructional model and pilot with several units.

- Start with the goal of developing curiosity and interest, asking, "What already promotes student curiosity and interest? What would we need to do to develop greater student curiosity and interest?" Research potentially effective approaches to develop curiosity and interest, and begin introducing new methods as a pilot project.

- Map and analyze the current curriculum using the twelve lifelong learning criteria.

- Strengthen parts of the curriculum. For example, in the elementary grades, strengthen social studies and science units by adopting or designing a strong curriculum in each area.

- Incorporate more diverse readings, fiction and nonfiction, in the elementary grades, and begin using the four phases of instruction to integrate these readings into the curriculum.

- Incorporate a few open-ended assignments into units for writing and discussion.

- Change the methods of assessing students by including one or more of the following: open-ended assignments, performance tasks, projects, visual tools, and self-reflections.

- Introduce the interactive notebook as a way to upgrade student assignments and assessments.

- Introduce portfolios as a way of beginning to collect multiple types of data from students.

- Begin incorporating more writing assignments that provide students with more feedback and improvement mechanisms.

Step Two: Build the Foundation

Consider the following.

Determine and Share What Is Currently In Place

Determine the current strengths of the school or classroom program with respect to lifelong learning characteristics. What's working? Share strategies that are making a difference, pilot them in other situations, and regularly discuss the results.

Research, Pilot, and Incorporate New Strategies

Select one of the beginning implementation plan steps developed in the setting-the-stage phase. Conduct research to find out more about the implementation step and methods. For example, if the plan is to reduce the amount of content for each unit and focus each unit around essential questions and understandings, learn more about essential questions and understandings and find examples. Based on this research, pilot new approaches and strategies. Once you are comfortable with an implementation step, consider other steps. For example, if the first step is approaching instruction using the four phases, move next to new assessment approaches after successfully implementing the phases. Continue this process until many of the lifelong learning education practices are in place.

Revisit and Reexamine the Mission, Vision, Outcomes, and Implementation Plan

Periodically revisit and reevaluate the mission, vision, and outcomes to determine if you need to make changes. Recognize that as changes are implemented and errors and mistakes occur, there will be a need to revisit and rethink the mission and vision statement and improve and update the implementation plan.

Step Three: Deepen Learning

Consider the following.

Pilot, Implement, and Continue to Refine Ideas and Practices

At this point, many of the lifelong learning education practices are already in place, so now is the time to refine and extend current lifelong learning education practices and pilot new ideas to improve practice.

Develop Original Ideas for Implementing Lifelong Learning

Begin developing new strategies and approaches to expand on or personalize life-long learning education practices. Pilot and implement new ideas.

Share With and Learn From Others

Work collaboratively with others. Observe what others are doing in their class-rooms to implement lifelong learning goals and practices. Hold brainstorming ses-sions to consider new ways of implementation. Discuss individual students and their successes and challenges.

Step Four: Provide Closure

Consider the following.

Continue to Refine the Mission, Vision, and Practices

Lifelong learning education practices are now the norm, and lifelong learning edu-cation is the embedded focus of teaching and learning. Continue to refine the mis-sion, vision, and practices based on new ideas, new circumstances, and new input.

*Communicate and Share Ideas and Best Practices
With Others*

As expertise is developed in implementing a lifelong learning education, the new mission, vision, ideas, and practices are shared with others in presentations, exhibits, visits, websites, and in other ways.

Helpful Websites

Many websites are available to educators who wish to learn more about how to create school reform and innovative practices.

- Bob Pearlman at **www.bobpearlman.org**

- Jim Collins at **www.jimcollins.com/article_topics /articles.html**

Visit **go.SolutionTree.com/21stcenturyskills**
for live links to these and other resources.

Reflections—Chapter 6

The following questions and activities should provoke and stimulate thought and discussion about the vision for and implementation of lifelong learning.

- Write a haiku that depicts one or more of the key ideas of a lifelong learning education. A haiku is a Japanese poetry form that uses words and syllables to capture ideas and create a picture in the reader's mind. It consists of three lines, each line with a specified number of syllables. Line one contains five syllables, the second line contains seven, and the third contains five. Two examples that illustrate haiku poetry about lifelong learning follow.

    Change education
    Make it for lifelong learning
    Help our children thrive.

    Questions start me off
    Then I grow my learning and
    Enjoy more of school.

- Review the two scenarios that illustrate a teacher's movement toward a lifelong learning educational approach. In your opinion, what is realistic and workable about these scenarios? How do they help to suggest a change process?

- Review and reflect on the four change principles of highly successful organizations described in this chapter (page 161). What do these change principles suggest for designing professional development experiences for individual teachers, teacher teams, or schools?

Action Steps—Chapter 6

Consider taking the following action steps to improve lifelong learning instruction.

- Write an advice column for teachers that responds to the following request from a teacher. Post the column or share with others if appropriate.

  My students show little interest in what I am teaching, and I am concerned that they are not learning what is important or retaining their learning. How do I solve these problems? What should I do differently?

- Use the reproducible "Lifelong Learning Education Analysis" (page 183) to identify the current program's strengths and the challenges of implementing a lifelong learning education program. Then use the reproducible "Designing a Lifelong Learning Education Professional Development Plan" (page 180) to develop an action plan that puts these recommendations into effect.

Designing a Lifelong Learning Education Professional Development Plan

Use the professional development phases and steps listed here to develop a plan for implementing a lifelong learning education. Pick and choose which steps to implement and describe what activities you will complete during implementation.

Professional Development Phases and Steps	Activities
Phase One—Setting the Stage	
Develop an initial understanding of what a lifelong learning education means.	
Pose and discuss initial essential questions.	
Create a lifelong learning education mission and vision.	
Explore the student outcome implications of a lifelong learning education.	
Analyze current lifelong learning education strengths and obstacles.	
Develop an initial implementation plan.	

page 1 of 2

Phase Two—Building the Foundation	
Determine and share what is currently in place.	
Research, pilot, and begin to incorporate new strategies.	
Revisit and reexamine the mission, vision, outcomes, and implementation plan.	
Phase Three—Deepening Learning	
Pilot, implement, and continue to refine ideas and practices begun in phase two.	
Develop original ideas for implementing a lifelong learning education.	
Share with and learn from others.	
Phase Four—Providing Closure	
Continue refining the mission, vision, and practices.	
Communicate and share ideas and best practices with others.	

page 2 of 2

Planning Tool for Creating a Mission and Vision Statement

For each of the four categories listed in the left column, develop a list of practices in the middle column. Then, in the Suggested Changes column, for each category, indicate the lifelong learning education areas that you would like to work on and improve in the future.

Educational Category	Current Practices	Suggested Changes
Educational goals		
Instructional practices		
Assessment practices		
Curriculum		

Lifelong Learning Education Analysis

When considering what changes to implement for a successful lifelong learning education program, review the following goals and then record, either alone or with a team, what strengths and challenges your school faces making them. Determine what should occur first and record that in the Suggested Priority Changes column.

Topic	Analysis of Strengths and Challenges	Suggested Priority Changes
Lifelong learning goals: • Develop curious explorers and a growth mindset. • Promote understanding over learning discrete facts and information. • Teach the core lifelong learning skills. • Encourage students' growth mindset. • Promote deeper learning experiences and independent and interdependent learning. • Broaden and enrich student learning.		

Lifelong learning instruction:
 	
• Implement the four phases.
  ◇ Phase one—setting the stage
  ◇ Phase two—building the foundation
  ◇ Phase three—deepening learning
  ◇ Phase four—providing closure
• Use multiple, engaging activities and strategies.
• Use the principle of research-based learning.
• Ensure productive struggle and independent learning.
• Promote learning progressions over time.		

page 1 of 2

Topic	Analysis of Strengths and Challenges	Suggested Priority Changes
Lifelong learning assessment: • Include diagnostic, formative, and summative assessments. • Incorporate a variety of lifelong learning assessments. • Provide students with feedback that improves their learning and their work over time.		

Lifelong learning curriculum:
 • Use the twelve lifelong learning curriculum criteria for the following.
   ◇ Map and analyze the current curriculum.
   ◇ Select and adopt new curricula.
 • Modify the curriculum using the UbD model.		

Project-based learning and civics education • Incorporate project-based learning on a regular basis. • Implement a strong civics education program.		

*Some general activities are useful for both instruction and assessment.

page 2 of 2

Teaching for Lifelong Learning © 2021 Elliott Seif • SolutionTree.com
Visit **go.SolutionTree.com/21stcenturyskills** to download this free reproducible.

Epilogue

Changing tomorrow starts today.

—Unknown

I began this book by describing a child who loves to play video games and learns how to play them well. That child starts with an interest in and curiosity about gaming and begins at a level of learning that is challenging but also possible. As this child moves through the game's levels, the challenges become greater, understanding of the game grows, strategies become more complex, and reflexes improve. As the player sticks with it, interest grows along with expertise.

School learning—preparation for lifelong learning—should be like developing expertise playing a video game. For all students it should, over time, lead to a progressively higher level of learning that raises the standard of excellence, leads to greater understanding, improves complex learning skills, develops the ability to work independently and interdependently, and grows talents and abilities. At the same time, school learning should actively engage students, promote and enhance curiosity, and create a growth mindset that fosters the desire to continue learning and improving during and beyond K–12 schooling.

But this way of thinking about education, these types of changes, will only be put into practice if educators value their worth and usefulness and themselves develop a growth mindset. Implementation ultimately comes down to the intentions, goals, skills, and values of educators. For example, if a teacher values student curiosity, and thus is open to finding ways to encourage it, he will develop classroom approaches that support student curiosity. If a teacher values building a foundation of lifelong learning understandings and skills, she will find ways to develop student understanding and make room for developing the lifelong learning skills identified in chapter 1 (page 17). If a teacher values research-based learning instead of relying solely on textbooks, that educator will find ways to introduce multiple sources of readings and student research opportunities. If a teacher values deepening learning, that educator will create learning opportunities that enable students to work independently and interdependently.

Implementing a lifelong learning education approach also means that teachers value greater student engagement and thus communicate often with students, listen to their ideas and ways of thinking, discover their interests, and work with them to determine what questions they would like to study. They value student opinions. Teachers take the time to diagnose prior student learning and use that information to structure their approaches. They encourage students to search for resources, ask questions as they learn, and find answers to questions on their own. They use feedback strategies to determine whether students understand what is being taught and to help them improve their work. They learn how to work with students as partners in the learning process.

While lifelong learning goals and practices are meaningful and important, they are also complex and challenging to implement. Effective, long-lasting changes to classrooms, schools, and districts are more likely to happen if there is a positive culture that supports change, such as time devoted to exploring new ideas and practices, funding that helps put new ideas into practice, a pat on the back for good work, and financial rewards for good teaching.

Moving toward an education that supports lifelong learning is often slow and challenging. Changes should be implemented gradually and carefully, and slowly gain momentum over time. Jim Collins (2019) calls this the *flywheel effect*:

> In creating a good-to-great transformation, there is no single defining action, no grand program, no single killer innovation, no solitary lucky break, no miracle moment. Rather, it feels like turning a giant, heavy flywheel. Pushing with great effort, you get the flywheel to inch forward. You keep pushing, and with persistent effort, you get the flywheel to complete an entire turn. You don't stop, you keep pushing. The flywheel moves a bit faster. Two turns . . . then four . . . then eight . . . the flywheel builds momentum . . . sixteen . . . thirty-two . . . moving faster . . . Then at some point—breakthrough! The flywheel flies forward with almost unstoppable momentum. (p. 1)

Focusing on one or two changes at a time is critical for successfully and carefully getting the flywheel moving (Schmoker, 2019). Individual teachers, teacher teams, schools, and districts can use the guidelines for change principles, and the four-phase professional development model suggested in chapter 6 (page 159), to gradually implement changes that move toward lifelong learning. Ultimately, the goal is to raise the level of student learning over time in order to prepare students for a changing, challenging, and uncertain world. Each step along the way is helpful. Each will make a difference.

Here are some questions to answer along the way.

- Where are you now?

- Where would you like to be?

- How will you get there?

- What's realistic and doable?

- Who are your allies? Who can be helpful?

There are no shortcuts. The teaching journey that rethinks the way we educate students requires patience, resilience, and trial and error. But we also need to remember that we can only get there if we move forward slowly and carefully, one step at a time.

As this ancient Lao Tzu saying tells us, "A journey of a thousand miles begins with a single step" (Lao Tzu, as cited in BBC Learning English, n.d.).

References and Resources

Adler, M. (2011, December 10). *Reconstituting the Constitution: How to rewrite it?* Accessed at https://npr .org/2011/12/10/143354018/reconstituting-the-constitution-how-to-rewrite-it on July 9, 2020.

American Association of School Librarians. (2018). *AASL standards framework for learners* [Pamphlet]. Accessed at https://standards.aasl.org/wp-content/uploads/2017/11/AASL-Standards -Framework-for-Learners-pamphlet.pdf on July 9, 2020.

Anderson, M. (2016). *Learning to choose, choosing to learn: The key to student motivation and achievement.* Alexandria, VA: Association for Supervision and Curriculum Development.

Arter, J., & McTighe, J. (2001). *Scoring rubrics in the classroom: Using performance criteria for assessing and improving student performance.* Thousand Oaks, CA: Corwin Press.

Barell, J. (2003). *Developing more curious minds.* Alexandria, VA: Association for Supervision and Curriculum Development.

Barell, J. (2006). *Problem-based learning: An inquiry approach* (2nd ed.). Thousand Oaks, CA: Corwin Press.

Barnas, B., Sumarmo, U., & Syaban, M. (2018). *The role of SQ3R strategy on mathematical communication ability and self regulated learning of seventh grade student.* Accessed at https://journal.ikipsiliwangi .ac.id/index.php/jiml/article/view/2199/260 on August 22, 2020.

Barry, T. (2018, June 4). *PBL in music: Driving questions invoke deeper musical learning* [Blog post]. Accessed at https://pblworks.org/blog/pbl-music-driving-questions-invoke-deeper-musical -learning on July 9, 2020.

BBC Learning English. (n.d.). *Lao Tzu.* Accessed at www.bbc.co.uk/worldservice/learningenglish /movingwords/shortlist/laotzu.shtml on January 2, 2021.

Beers, S., & Howell, L. (2003). *Reading strategies for the content areas: An ASCD action tool* (Vol. 1). Alexandria, VA: Association for Supervision and Curriculum Development.

Berger, R. (2003). *An ethic of excellence: Building a culture of craftsmanship with students.* Portsmouth, NH: Heinemann.

Berger, R., Woodfin, L., & Vilen, A. (2016). *Learning that lasts: Challenging, engaging, and empowering students with deeper instruction.* San Francisco: Jossey-Bass.

Blackburn, B. R. (2018). *Productive struggle is a learner's sweet spot.* Accessed at www.ascd.org/ascd-express /vol14/num11/productive-struggle-is-a-learners-sweet-spot.aspx on January 2, 2021.

Block, J. (2020). *Teaching for a living democracy: Project-based learning in the English and history classroom.* New York: Teachers College Press.

Bloom, B. S. (1986). Automaticity: "The hands and feet of genius." *Educational Leadership, 43*(5), 70–77.

Boss, S., & Larmer, J. (2018). *Project based teaching: How to create rigorous and engaging learning experiences.* Alexandria, VA: Association for Supervision and Curriculum Development.

Brain Wrinkles. (2013). *Interactive social studies notebooks.* Accessed at www.richmond.k12.nc.us /view/5285.pdf on July 13, 2020.

Bransford, J. D., Brown, A. L., & Cocking, R. R. (Eds.). (1999). *How people learn: Brain, mind, experience, and school.* Washington, DC: National Academies Press.

Bratslavsky, L., Wright, A., Kritselis, A., & Luftig, D. (2019). The strategically ambiguous assignment: An approach to promoting critical and creative thinking in visual communication. *Journal of Visual Literacy, 38*(4), 285–304.

Briggs, S. (2014, July 12). *How to take notes: Learning from the strategies that set straight-A students apart.* Accessed at www.opencolleges.edu.au/informed/features/how-to-take-notes-strategies on August 23, 2020.

Brookhart, S. M. (2013). *How to create and use rubrics for formative assessment and grading.* Alexandria, VA: Association for Supervision and Curriculum Development.

Brookhart, S. M., & Nitko, A. J. (2008). *Assessment and grading in classrooms.* London: Pearson.

Burz, H. L., & Marshall, K. (1996). *Performance-based curriculum for mathematics: From knowing to showing.* Thousand Oaks, CA: Corwin Press.

Burz, H. L., & Marshall, K. (1997a). *Performance-based curriculum for language arts: From knowing to showing.* Thousand Oaks, CA: Corwin Press.

Burz, H. L., & Marshall, K. (1997b). *Performance-based curriculum for science: From knowing to showing.* Thousand Oaks, CA: Corwin Press.

Burz, H. L., & Marshall, K. (1998). *Performance-based curriculum for social studies: From knowing to showing.* Thousand Oaks, CA: Corwin Press.

C3 Teachers. (n.d.). *The inquiry design model.* Accessed at www.c3teachers.org/inquiry-design-model on July 13, 2020.

California Department of Education. (2000, May 18). *History–social science content standards for California public schools, kindergarten through grade twelve.* Accessed at www.cde.ca.gov/be/st/ss /documents/histsocscistnd.pdf on September 11, 2020.

California Polytechnic State University. (n.d.). *Note taking systems.* Accessed at https://asc.calpoly.edu/ssl/ notetakingsystems on March 3, 2021.

Calkins, L., & Mermelstein, L. (2003). *Launching the writing workshop.* Portsmouth, NH: FirstHand.

Center for Civic Education. (n.d.). *We the people textbook series for upper elementary, middle and secondary schools.* Accessed at www.civiced.org/teaching-resources on August 11, 2020.

Chien, Y., & Morris, P. (2017, April 11). *Is U.S. manufacturing really declining?* [Blog post]. Accessed at https://stlouisfed.org/on-the-economy/2017/april/us-manufacturing-really-declining on July 13, 2020.

Cohen, B. (2013, February 26). *PFT negotiations have begun* [Blog post]. Accessed at www.bncohen.com /making-the-grade-blog/archives/02-2013 on August 11, 2020.

Collins, J. (2019). *Turning the flywheel: A monograph to accompany* Good to Great. New York: Harper Business.

Collins, J., & Hansen, M. T. (2011). *Great by choice: Uncertainty, chaos, and luck—Why some thrive despite them all.* New York: Harper Business.

Colvin, G. (2008). *Talent is overrated: What really separates world-class performers from everybody else.* New York: Portfolio.

Comprehension Connection. (n.d.). *Fourteen activators that will give your lessons pop.* Accessed at www .comprehensionconnection.net/2019/01/fourteen-activators-that-will-give-your.html on January 25, 2021.

Conley, D. T. (2010). *College and career ready: Helping all students succeed beyond high school.* San Francisco: Jossey-Bass.

Copeland, M. (2005). *Socratic circles: Fostering critical and creative thinking in middle and high school.* Portland, ME: Stenhouse.

Costa, A. L. (Ed.). (2001). *Developing minds: A resource book for teaching thinking* (3rd ed.). Alexandria, VA: Association for Supervision and Curriculum Development.

Costa, A. L., & Kallick, B. (Eds.). (2000). *Discovering and exploring habits of mind.* Alexandria, VA: Association for Supervision and Curriculum Development.

Costa, A. L., & Kallick, B. (Eds.). (2008). *Leading and learning with habits of mind: 16 essential characteristics for success.* Alexandria, VA: Association for Supervision and Curriculum Development.

Dabrowski, J., & Marshall, T. R. (2018). *Motivation and engagement in student assignments: The role of choice and relevancy.* Accessed at https://files.eric.ed.gov/fulltext/ED593328.pdf on September 2, 2020.

Daggett, W. R. (2016). *Rigor/Relevance Framework: A guide to focusing resources to increase student performance* [White paper]. Rexford, NY: International Center for Leadership in Education. Accessed at https://leadered.com/wp-content/uploads/Rigor-Relevance-Framework-White-Paper-2016-1.pdf on August 26, 2020.

Darling-Hammond, L. (2011). Soaring systems: High flyers all have equitable funding, shared curriculum, and quality teaching. *American Educator, 34*(4), 20–23.

Darling-Hammond, L., & Adamson, F. (2010). *Beyond basic skills: The role of performance assessment in achieving 21st century standards of learning* [Research brief]. Stanford, CA: Stanford Center for Opportunity Policy in Education. Accessed at https://edpolicy.stanford.edu/sites/default/files/beyond-basic-skills-role-performance-assessment-achieving-21st-century-standards-learning-executive-summary_0.pdf on August 26, 2020.

de Bono, E. (1985). *Six thinking hats.* Boston: Little, Brown.

Dean, C., Hubbell, E. R., Pitler, H., & Stone, B. (2012). *Classroom instruction that works: Research-based strategies for increasing student achievement* (2nd ed.). Alexandria, VA: Association for Supervision and Curriculum Development.

Delta Education. (n.d.). *FOSS next generation K–8.* Accessed at https://deltaeducation.com/foss/next-generation on July 13, 2020.

Dickens, C. (1992). *Oliver Twist.* New York: W. W. Norton & Company. (Original work published 1837–1839)

Dimich, N. (2014). *Design in five: Essential phases to create engaging assessment practice.* Bloomington, IN: Solution Tree Press.

Dougherty, K. (2008). *I didn't know that was poetry [8th grade].* Accessed at https://digitalcommons.trinity.edu/educ_understandings/60 on November 18, 2020.

DuFour, R., DuFour, R., Eaker, R., Many, T. W., & Mattos, M. (2016). *Learning by doing: A handbook for Professional Learning Communities at Work.* Bloomington, IN: Solution Tree Press.

Dweck, C. S. (2006). *Mindset: The new psychology of success.* New York: Random House.

Dweck, C. S. (2015). *Carol Dweck revisits the "growth mindset."* Accessed at www.edweek.org/ew/articles/2015/09/23/carol-dweck-revisits-the-growth-mindset.html on August 23, 2020.

Education Week. (n.d.). *Special report: Projects, portfolios, and performance assessments—Exploring alternatives to traditional tests.* Accessed at http://bit.ly/38GTjv7 on July 15, 2020.

Educational Testing Service. (1993). *Letter writing assessment: Teacher directions.* Princeton, NJ: Author.

Eichner, J. A., & Bacon, B. (1964). *The first book of local government.* New York: F. Watts.

EiE, Boston Museum of Science. (n.d.). *About engineering adventures.* Accessed at www.eie.org/engineering-adventures/about-engineering-adventures on July 13, 2020.

ENC Focus. (2002, November 2). Task by Robert E. Freeman, Public Schools of Robeson County, Lumberton, North Carolina. *Eisenhower National Clearinghouse, 9,* 16–18.

EngageNY. (n.d.). *New York State K–12 social studies resource toolkit.* Accessed at www.engageny.org/resource/new-york-state-k-12-social-studies-resource-toolkit on July 13, 2020.

Engel, S. (2013). The case for curiosity. *Educational Leadership*, *70*(5), 36–40.

Esquith, R. (2003). *There are no shortcuts.* New York: Pantheon Books.

FairTest. (2019, May). *Graduation test update: States that recently eliminated or scaled back high school exit exams.* Accessed at https://fairtest.org/graduation-test-update-states-recently-eliminated on July 13, 2020.

Fendel, D., Resek, D., Alper, L., & Fraser, S. (n.d.). *Interactive Mathematics Program (IMP).* Accessed at www.activatelearning.com/interactive-mathematics-program-imp on July 13, 2020.

Fisher, D., & Frey, N. (2014). *Checking for understanding: Formative assessment techniques for your classroom* (2nd ed.). Alexandria, VA: Association for Supervision and Curriculum Development.

Flipped Learning Network. (2014, March 12). *Definition of flipped learning.* Accessed at www.flippedlearning.org/definition on July 13, 2020.

Fogarty, R. J., Kerns, G. M., & Pete, B. M. (2020). *Literacy reframed: How a focus on decoding, vocabulary, and background knowledge improves reading comprehension.* Bloomington, IN: Solution Tree Press.

Fraser, C. (2018). *Love the questions: Reclaiming research with curiosity and passion.* Portsmouth, NH: Stenhouse.

Gallagher, K. (2004). *Deeper reading: Comprehending challenging texts, 4–12.* Portland, ME: Stenhouse.

Garan, E. M., & Devoogd, G. (2008). The benefits of sustained silent reading: Scientific research and common sense converge. *Reading Teacher*, *62*(4), 336–344.

Gardner, H. (1991). *The unschooled mind: How children think and how schools should teach.* New York: Basic Books.

Gardner, T. (2005). *Traci's 34th list of ten: Ten tips for designing writing assignments* [Blog post]. Accessed at www.tengrrl.com/tens/034.shtml on July 13, 2020.

Gardoqui, K. E. (2018). We spend too much time teaching students to argue. *Education Week*, *38*(7), 20.

Ginsberg, A. E. (2012). *Embracing risk in urban education: Curiosity, creativity, and courage in the era of "no excuses" and relay race reform.* Lanham, MD: Rowman and Littlefield Education.

Ginsburg, D. (2015, February 28). *Do more for students by doing less for students* [Blog post]. Accessed at http://blogs.edweek.org/teachers/coach_gs_teaching_tips/2015/02/do_more _for_students_by_doing_less_for_students.html on July 13, 2020.

Gladwell, M. (2000). *The tipping point: How little things can make a big difference.* Boston: Little, Brown.

Gonchar, M. (2014, October 7). *Fifty ways to teach with current events* [Blog post]. Accessed at https:// learning.blogs.nytimes.com/2014/10/07/50-ways-to-teach-current-events on July 13, 2020.

Gould, J. (Ed.). (n.d.). *Guardian of democracy: The civic mission of schools.* Accessed at https://production -carnegie.s3.amazonaws.com/filer_public/ab/dd/abdda62e-6e84-47a4-a043-348d2f2085ae /ccny_grantee_2011_guardian.pdf on July 13, 2020.

Grant, A., & Grant, A. S. (2020, September 7). Kids can learn to love learning, even over Zoom. *The New York Times*. Accessed at www.nytimes.com/2020/09/07/opinion/remote-school.html on November 27, 2020.

Green, P. (Ed.). (2000). *Graphic organizer collection*. San Antonio, TX: Novel Units.

Grodin, E. (2004). *D is for democracy: A citizen's alphabet*. Chelsea, MI: Sleeping Bear Press.

Haroutunian-Gordon, S. (2014). *Interpretive discussion: Engaging students in text-based conversations*. Cambridge, MA: Harvard Education Press.

Hasso Plattner Institute of Design at Stanford University. (n.d.). *About*. Accessed at https://dschool.stanford.edu/about on July 13, 2020.

Hattie, J. (2012). *Visible learning for teachers: Maximizing impact on learning*. New York: Routledge.

Heick, T. (2019, May 13). *A giant list of really good essential questions* [Blog post]. Accessed at https://teachthought.com/pedagogy/examples-of-essential-questions on July 14, 2020.

Hellerich, K. (2020). *Using retakes to nurture growth mindset*. Accessed at www.edutopia.org/article/using-retakes-nurture-growth-mindset#:~:text=With%20a%20growth%20mindset%2C%20students,yet.&text=When%20applied%20in%20a%20classroom,mindset%20approach%20helps%20students%20progress on January 5, 2021.

Himmele, P., & Himmele, W. (2017). *Total participation techniques: Making every student an active learner* (2nd ed.). Alexandria, VA: Association for Supervision and Curriculum Development.

Hirsch, E. D., Jr. (2016). *Why knowledge matters: Rescuing our children from failed educational theories*. Cambridge, MA: Harvard Education Press.

Huguet, A., Kavanagh, J., Baker, G., & Blumenthal, M. S. (2019). *Exploring media literacy education as a tool for mitigating truth decay*. Santa Monica, CA: RAND.

Hyerle, D. (1996). *Visual tools for constructing knowledge*. Alexandria, VA: Association for Supervision and Curriculum Development.

Hyerle, D. (2009). *Visual tools for transforming information into knowledge* (2nd ed.). Thousand Oaks, CA: Corwin Press.

International Baccalaureate. (n.d.). *Benefits for schools*. Accessed at www.ibo.org/benefits/benefits-for-schools on August 12, 2020.

Isaksen, S. G., Dorval, K. B., & Treffinger, D. J. (1994). *Creative approaches to problem solving*. Dubuque, IA: Kendall-Hunt.

Jacobs, H. H. (1997). *Mapping the big picture: Integrating curriculum and assessment, K–12*. Alexandria, VA: Association for Supervision and Curriculum Development.

Jacobs, H. H. (2010a). *Curriculum mapping 101* [Presentation]. Accessed at www.curriculum21.com/z-docs/CMpresentation.pdf on January 2, 2021.

Jacobs, H. H. (Ed.). (2010b). *Curriculum21: Essential education for a changing world*. Alexandria, VA: Association for Supervision and Curriculum Development.

Jacobs, H. H., & Alcock, M. H. (2017). *Bold moves for schools: How we create remarkable learning environments*. Alexandria, VA: Association for Supervision and Curriculum Development.

Jacobs, H. H., & Johnson, A. (2009). *The curriculum mapping planner: Templates, tools, and resources for effective professional development*. Alexandria, VA: Association for Supervision and Curriculum Development.

JASON Learning. (n.d.). *About us*. Accessed at https://jason.org/about on July 16, 2020.

Karpova, E., Marcketti, S. B., & Barker, J. (2011). The efficacy of teaching creativity: Assessment of student creative thinking before and after exercises. *Clothing and Textiles Research Journal, 29*(1), 52–66.

Katz, L. G., Chard, S. C., & Kogan, Y. (2014). *Engaging children's minds: The project approach* (3rd ed.). Santa Barbara, CA: Praeger.

Kay, K. (2017, May 12). *The graduate profile: A focus on outcomes*. Accessed at www.edutopia.org/blog/graduate-profile-focus-outcomes-ken-kay on January 5, 2021.

Kelly, M. (2019, July 29). *The pros and cons of block schedules* [Blog post]. Accessed at https://thoughtco.com/class-block-scheduling-pros-and-cons-6460 on July 13, 2020.

Kim, H., & Care, E. (2018, March 27). *Learning progressions: Pathways for 21st century teaching and learning* [Blog post]. Accessed at https://brookings.edu/blog/education-plus-development/2018/03/27/learning-progressions-pathways-for-21st-century-teaching-and-learning on July 13, 2020.

Kuijk, A. (2017, September 27). *SQ3R method*. Accessed at www.toolshero.com/personal-development/sq3r-method on August 12, 2020.

Larmer, J., Mergendoller, J., & Boss, S. (2015). *Setting the standard for project based learning: A proven approach to rigorous classroom instruction*. Alexandria, VA: Association for Supervision and Curriculum Development.

Larmer, J., Ross, D., & Mergendoller, J. R. (2009). *PBL starter kit: To-the-point advice, tools and tips for your first project*. Novato, CA: Buck Institute for Education.

Lee, L. (2019, June 25). *Teaching students how to ask productive questions* [Blog post]. Accessed at https://edut.to/2OhrC6g on July 13, 2020.

Lenter, K. (2012). Enhancing and displacing literacy practices: Examining student publishing in a fifth grade writer's workshop. *Language and Literacy, 14*(1), 125–151.

Lester, J. (2016). *The passion project: A teacher's guide for implementing passion projects in your classroom*. Marion, IL: Pieces of Learning.

Letter, T. (2016). *Bringing joy to the classroom with passion projects: Five steps to enhance learning in the classroom*. Accessed at https://creativeeducator.tech4learning.com/2016/articles/passion-projects on July 13, 2020.

Littky, D. (2004). *The big picture: Education is everyone's business*. Alexandria, VA: Association for Supervision and Curriculum Development.

Luman, R. (2001). *The writing process: Steps in writing an essay*. Accessed at www.beulah.k12.nd.us/cms/lib/ND01911222/Centricity/Domain/103/9301_9056_attach_3988.pdf on July 13, 2020.

MacArthur Research Network on Youth and Participatory Politics. (2018). *Digital civics toolkit.* Accessed at https://digitalcivicstoolkit.org on July 13, 2020.

Marcarelli, K. (2010). *Teaching science with interactive notebooks.* Thousand Oaks, CA: Corwin Press.

Markham, T. (2012). *Project based learning: Design and coaching guide.* San Rafael, CA: HeartIQ Press.

Marzano, R. J. (2003). *What works in schools: Translating research into action.* Alexandria, VA: Association for Supervision and Curriculum Development.

Marzano, R. J. (2004). *Building background knowledge for academic achievement: Research on what works in schools.* Alexandria, VA: Association for Supervision and Curriculum Development.

Marzano, R. J. (2019). *The handbook for the new art and science of teaching.* Bloomington, IN: Solution Tree Press.

Mazur, E. (1997). *Peer instruction: A user's manual.* Upper Saddle River, NJ: Prentice Hall.

McCarthy, J. (2018). *Extending the silence.* Accessed at www.edutopia.org/article/extending-silence on September 2, 2020.

McKnight, K. S. (2010). *The teacher's big book of graphic organizers: 100 reproducible organizers that help kids with reading, writing, and the content areas.* San Francisco: Jossey-Bass.

McKnight, K. S. (2013). *The elementary teacher's big book of graphic organizers: 100+ ready-to-use organizers that help kids learn language arts, science, social studies, and more!* San Francisco: Jossey-Bass.

McTighe, J. (2011, January). *Measuring what matters: Part 1—The case for an assessment overhaul.* Accessed at www.ceelcenter.org/wordpress/wp-content/uploads/2016/06/Measuring-What-Matters.pdf on August 12, 2020.

McTighe, J., Doubet, K. J., & Carbaugh, E. M. (2020). *Designing authentic performance tasks and projects: Tools for meaningful learning and assessment.* Alexandria, VA: Association for Supervision and Curriculum Development.

McTighe, J., & Lyman, F. T. (1988). Cueing thinking in the classroom: The promise of theory-embedded tools. *Educational Leadership, 45*(7), 18.

McTighe, J., & O'Connor, K. (2005). *Seven practices for effective learning.* Accessed at http://courses.edtechleaders.org/documents/seven_practices.pdf on January 5, 2021.

McTighe, J., & Seif, E. (2010). An implementation framework to support 21st century skills. In J. Bellanca & R. Brandt (Eds.), *21st century skills: Rethinking how students learn* (pp. 149–172). Bloomington, IN: Solution Tree Press.

McTighe, J., & Silver, H. F. (2020). *Teaching for deeper learning: Tools to engage students in meaning making.* Alexandria, VA: Association for Supervision and Curriculum Development.

McTighe, J., & Wiggins, G. (2013). *Essential questions: Opening doors to student understanding.* Alexandria, VA: Association for Supervision and Curriculum Development.

Mehta, J., & Fine, S. (2019). *In search of deeper learning: The quest to remake the American high school.* Cambridge, MA: Harvard University Press.

Meiser, E. (2016). *6 best mind mapping tools for creative students*. Accessed at https://elearningindustry .com/6-best-mind-mapping-tools-creative-students on January 25, 2021.

Miller, A. (2017, December 21). *A more complete picture of student learning* [Blog post]. Accessed at https://edutopia.org/article/more-complete-picture-student-learning on July 13, 2020.

Mineo, L. (2019, August 23). *Searching for deeper learning: A recipe for how high schools can foster more analytical, critical, and creative thinking*. Accessed at https://news.harvard.edu /gazette/story/2019/08/a-recipe-for-how-high-schools-can-foster-deeper-learning/?utm _source=SilverpopMailing&utm_medium=email&utm_campaign=Daily%20Gazette%20 20190826%20(1) on July 13, 2020.

Minero, E. (2018, June 18). *Driving deep reading comprehension in K–5* [Blog post]. Accessed at https:// edut.to/2JSDAPD on July 13, 2020.

Mohamad, A. M., Mustafa, E., Hanafiah, N. A. H., Ariffin, N. M., & Arshad, A. H. M. (2019). *Impact of "think-pair-share" and "wait-time" on teaching and learning undergraduates: An action research*. Accessed at https://pdfs.semanticscholar.org/c027/bda50b526d7bd5dcab19f6ad512da8b14349 .pdf on September 2, 2020.

Moretti, E. (2013). *The new geography of jobs*. Boston: Mariner Books.

Natanson, H. (2020, January 20). *This teacher raised money for 1,000 books so her students would learn to love reading*. Accessed at www.washingtonpost.com/local/education/this-virginia-educator -is-teaching-students-to-love-reading-she-paid-for-a-library-of-1000-books-by-raising-money -online/2020/01/19/fb409dac-36de-11ea-bb7b-265f4554af6d_story.html on August 12, 2020.

National Academies of Sciences, Engineering, and Medicine. (2018). *How people learn II: Learners, contexts, and cultures*. Accessed at https://doi.org/10.17226/24783 on July 13, 2020.

National Council for the Social Studies. (2010). *National Curriculum Standards for Social Studies: A framework for teaching, learning, and assessment* (Rev. ed.). Silver Spring, MD: Author.

National Council of Teachers of English. (2013). *Formative assessment that* truly *informs instruction*. Accessed at https://cdn.ncte.org/nctefiles/resources/positions/formative-assessment_single.pdf on January 5, 2021.

National Education Association. (n.d.). *K-W-L (know, want to know, learned)*. Accessed at www.nea.org /tools/k-w-l-know-want-to-know-learned.html on July 13, 2020.

National Human Genome Research Institute. (n.d.). *Human Genome Project results*. Accessed at www.genome.gov/human-genome-project/results on October 11, 2020.

National Research Council. (2005). *How students learn: History, mathematics, and science in the classroom*. Washington, DC: National Academies Press.

Nehring, J., Charner-Laird, M., & Szczesiul, S. (2017). What real high performance looks like. *Phi Delta Kappan*, *98*(7), 38–42.

Nevins, M. (2018, December 4). *How to collaborate with people you don't like*. Accessed at https://hbr .org/2018/12/how-to-collaborate-with-people-you-dont-like on July 13, 2020.

The New Teacher Project. (n.d.). *The opportunity myth: What students can show us about how school is letting them down—and how to fix it*. Accessed at https://opportunitymyth.tntp.org on July 14, 2020.

The New Teacher Project. (2019, April 25). *The weight of wasted time in school* [Blog post]. Accessed at https://tntp.org/blog/post/the-weight-of-wasted-time-in-school on July 14, 2020.

Newmann, F. (Ed.). (1996). *Authentic achievement: Restructuring schools for intellectual quality*. San Francisco: Jossey-Bass.

Newmann, F. M., Carmichael, D. L., & King, M. B. (2016). *Authentic intellectual work: Improving teaching for rigorous learning*. Thousand Oaks, CA: Corwin Press.

NGSS Lead States. (2013). *Next Generation Science Standards: For states, by states*. Washington, DC: National Academies Press. Accessed at www.nextgenscience.org/searchstandards on May 6, 2019.

O'Connor, K. (2002). *How to grade for learning: Linking grades to standards*. Thousand Oaks, CA: Corwin Press.

Ogle, D. (1986). K-W-L: A teaching model that develops active reading of expository text. *Reading Teacher, 39*, 564–570.

Olivares, S. (2012). *Interactive notebooks: Meeting the needs of English language learners*. Accessed at www.esc4.net/users/0205/inb_ell.pdf on January 25, 2021.

Orenstein, N. (2019, June 14). *The state of civics education in 2019* [Blog post]. Accessed at https://ewa.org/blog-educated-reporter/state-civics-education-2019 on July 13, 2020.

Paulson, F. L., Paulson, P. R., & Meyer, C. A. (1991). What makes a portfolio a portfolio? *Educational Leadership, 48*(5), 60–63. Accessed at https://web.stanford.edu/dept/SUSE/projects/ireport/articles/e-portfolio/what%20makes%20a%20portfolio%20a%20portfolio.pdf on August 27, 2020.

PBLWorks. (2019a). *Essential project design elements checklist*. Accessed at https://my.pblworks.org/resource/document/pbl_essential_elements_checklist on July 13, 2020.

PBLWorks. (2019b). *Gold standard PBL: Essential project design elements*. Accessed at https://my.pblworks.org/resource/document/gold_standard_pbl_essential_project_design_elements on July 13, 2020.

Peha, S. (2003). *Welcome to Writer's Workshop*. Accessed at http://ttms.org/PDFs/05%20Writers%20Workshop%20v001%20(Full).pdf on July 13, 2020.

Performance Assessment Resource Bank. (n.d.). *Welcome to the Performance Assessment Resource Bank*. Accessed at www.performanceassessmentresourcebank.org on August 4, 2020.

Perkins, D. N. (2014). *Future Wise: Educating our children for a changing world*. San Francisco: Jossey-Bass.

Phi Delta Kappa Poll. (2019, September). *51st annual PDK poll of the public's attitudes toward the public schools: Frustration in the schools—Teachers speak out on pay, funding, and feeling valued*. Accessed at https://pdkpoll.org/wp-content/uploads/2020/05/pdkpoll51-2019.pdf on July 14, 2020.

Philadelphia Higher Education Network for Neighborhood Development. (2005, February 25). *From classroom to citizen: American attitudes on civic education*. Accessed at www.phennd.org/update/from-classroom-to-citizen-american-attitudes-on-civic-education on July 13, 2020.

Pitler, H., Hubbell, E. R., & Kuhn, M. (2012). *Using technology with classroom instruction that works* (2nd ed.). Alexandria, VA: Association for Supervision and Curriculum Development.

Raths, L. E., Wasserman, S., Jonas, A., & Rothstein, A. M. (1986). *Teaching for thinking: Theory, strategies, and activities for the classroom* (2nd ed.). New York: Teachers College Press.

Recht, D. R., & Leslie, L. (1988). Effect of prior knowledge on good and poor readers' memory of text. *Journal of Educational Psychology, 80*(1), 16–20.

Regents of the University of California, Berkeley. (2016). *FOSS Program goals.* Accessed at www.fossweb .com/delegate/ssi-wdf-ucm-webContent?dDocName=G4302845 on August 12, 2020.

Renwick, M. (2017). *Digital portfolios in the classroom: Showcasing and assessing student work.* Alexandria, VA: Association for Supervision and Curriculum Development.

Reutzel, D. R., Jones, C. D., Fawson, P., & Smith, J. A. (2008). Scaffolded silent reading: A complement to guided repeated oral reading that works! *Reading Teacher, 62*(3), 194–207. Accessed at www.researchgate.net/publication/251810331_Scaffolded_Silent_Reading_A_Complement _to_Guided_Repeated_Oral_Reading_That_Works on August 28, 2020.

Ridgeway, E. (2014). *Interactive science notebooks* [Slideware presentation]. Accessed at www.liberty.k12 .ga.us/pdf/TandL/InteractiveNotebooks.pdf on September 16, 2020.

Right Question Institute. (n.d.). *Experiencing the Question Formulation Technique (QFT).* Accessed at www.ibmidatlantic.org/Experiencing-the-QFT.pdf on July 14, 2020.

Ritchhart, R., Church, M., & Morrison, K. (2011). *Making thinking visible: How to promote engagement, understanding, and independence for all learners.* San Francisco: Jossey-Bass.

Robinson, F. P. (1946). *Effective study.* New York: Harper & Brothers.

Roseth, C. J., Johnson, D. W., & Johnson, R. T. (2008). Promoting early adolescents' achievement and peer relationships: The effects of cooperative, competitive, and individualistic goal structures. *Psychological Bulletin, 134*(2), 223–246.

Rowe, M. B. (1986). Wait time: Slowing down may be a way of speeding up! *Journal of Teacher Education, 37*(1), 43–50.

Rutzler, S. (2020, February 2). *Importance of reading comprehension* [Blog post]. Accessed at www .mathgenie.com/blog/importance-of-reading-comprehension on August 23, 2020.

Sahm, C. (2017, January 10). *Why curriculum counts.* Accessed at https://edexcellence.net/articles/why -curriculum-counts on July 14, 2020.

Salzmann, M. E. (2003). *I am a good citizen.* Edina, MN: ABDO.

Samples, B. (1984, April). *Reflections on curriculum, teachers, and teaching.* Accessed at www.ascd.org /ASCD/pdf/journals/ed_lead/el_198404_samples.pdf on July 14, 2020.

Sampsel, A. (2013). *Finding the effects of think-pair-share on student confidence and participation.* Published dissertation, Bowling Green State University, Bowling Green, OH. Accessed at https://scholarworks.bgsu.edu/cgi/viewcontent.cgi?article=1029&context=honorsprojects on September 2, 2020.

Sandburg, C. (1916). *Chicago poems.* New York: Henry Holt and Company.

Saphier, J., & Haley, M. A. (1993a). *Activators: Activity structures to engage students' thinking before instruction.* Acton, MA: Research for Better Teaching.

Saphier, J., & Haley, M. A. (1993b). *Summarizers: Activity structures to support integration and retention of new learning.* Acton, MA: Research for Better Teaching.

Sawchuk, S. (2019, May 22). *Need a primer on Education Week's civics project? Listen to this EWA podcast* [Blog post]. Accessed at https://blogs.edweek.org/edweek/curriculum/2019/05/podcast _citizen_z_civics_education.html on July 14, 2020.

Schimmer, T. (2019). *Should formative assessments be graded?* [Blog post]. Accessed at www.solutiontree .com/blog/grading-formative-assessments/ on January 5, 2021.

Schmoker, M. (2018). *Focus: Elevating the essentials to radically improve student learning* (2nd ed.). Alexandria, VA: Association for Supervision and Curriculum Development.

Schmoker, M. (2019). Embracing the power of less. *Educational Leadership, 76*(6), 24–29.

Schoenbach, R., Greenleaf, C., Cziko, C., & Hurwitz, L. (1999). *Reading for understanding: A guide to improving reading in middle and high school classrooms.* San Francisco: Jossey-Bass.

Schrock, K. (n.d.). *Activators and summarizers* [Slideware presentation.]. Accessed at https://schrockguide .net/uploads/3/9/2/2/392267/schrock_activators.pdf on July 14, 2020.

Seif, E. (1977). *Teaching significant social studies in the elementary school.* Chicago: Rand McNally College.

Seif, E. (1993). Integrating skill development across the curriculum. *Schools in the Middle, 2*(4), 15–19.

Seif, E. (1998). *Curriculum renewal: A case study—A chapter of the curriculum handbook.* Alexandria, VA: Association for Supervision and Curriculum Development.

Shenk, D. (2010). *The genius in all of us: Why everything you've been told about genetics, talent, and IQ is wrong.* New York: Doubleday.

Silver, H. F., Strong, R. W., & Perini, M. J. (2007). *The strategic teacher: Selecting the right research-based strategy for every lesson.* Alexandria, VA: Association for Supervision and Curriculum Development.

Simon, C. A. (n.d.). *Strategy guide: Using the think-pair-share technique.* Accessed at www.readwritethink .org/professional-development/strategy-guides/using-think-pair-share-30626.html on July 14, 2020.

Slavin, R. E. (2014). Cooperative learning and academic achievement: Why does groupwork work? *Anales De Psicología, 30*(3), 785–791.

Small, M. (2006). *Being a good citizen.* Minneapolis, MN: Picture Window Books.

Smith, J. B., Lee, V. E., & Newmann, F. M. (2001, January). *Instruction and achievement in Chicago elementary schools.* Chicago: Consortium on Chicago School Research. Accessed at https:// consortium.uchicago.edu/sites/default/files/2018-10/p0f01.pdf on August 31, 2020.

Sobel, S. (2012). *How the U.S. government works . . . and how it all comes together to make a nation* (2nd ed.). Hauppauge, NY: Barron's.

Soots, B. (2020, February 9). *How politics plays out in textbooks* [Letter to the editor]. Accessed at www .nytimes.com/2020/02/08/opinion/letters/history-textbooks-politics.html on August 12, 2020.

St. George, D. (2019, August 5). *Student apprentices team up with school system's plumbers, carpenters, masons.* Accessed at https://wapo.st/2m169kf on July 14, 2020.

Stacy, E. M., & Cain, J. (2015). Note-taking and handouts in the digital age. *American Journal of Pharmaceutical Education, 79*(7). Accessed at www.ajpe.org/content/ajpe/79/7/107.full.pdf on August 23, 2020.

Stahl, R. J. (1994). *Using "think-time" and "wait-time" skillfully in the classroom.* Accessed at https://files .eric.ed.gov/fulltext/ED370885.pdf on September 2, 2020.

Stanford History Education Group. (n.d.). *Students are learning how to spot fake news.* Accessed at https:// sheg.stanford.edu on August 10, 2020.

Stanley, T. (2019). *Using rubrics for performance-based assessment: A practical guide to evaluating student work.* Waco, TX: Prufrock Press.

Sternberg, R. J. (2019). A theory of adaptive intelligence and its relation to general intelligence. *Journal of Intelligence, 7*(4), 23.

Stobaugh, R. (2019). *Fifty strategies to boost cognitive engagement: Creating a thinking culture in the classroom.* Bloomington, IN: Solution Tree Press.

Strauss, V. (2017, December 20). *The surprising thing Google learned about its employees—and what it means for today's students.* Accessed at https://wapo.st/2PAID9m on August 5, 2020.

Summit Public Schools. (n.d.). *Federalism today.* Accessed at https://iowacore.gov/sites/default/files /historyssfederalismtodaycomplexproject.pdf on July 14, 2020.

Sun, K. L. (2019, May 6). *Ditch the math worksheets and stop killing kids' curiosity* [Blog post]. Accessed at https://edweek.org/ew/articles/2019/05/08/ditch-the-math-worksheets-and-stop-killing.html on July 13, 2020.

Tanguay, M. (2020). *How to mind map to visualize ideas (with mind map examples).* Accessed at www .lifehack.org/articles/work/how-to-mind-map-in-three-small-steps.html on December 1, 2020.

Teachers' Curriculum Institute. (1999). *History alive! Six powerful teaching strategies: Manual for engaging all learners in the diverse classroom.* Mountain View, CA: Author.

Texas Education Agency. (1998). Chapter 110. Texas Essential Knowledge and Skills for English language arts and reading subchapter B—Middle school. Accessed at http://ritter.tea.state.tx.us/rules/tac/ chapter110/ch110b.html#110.24 on January 5, 2021.

Texas Education Agency. (2009). *Chapter 112. Texas Essential Knowledge and Skills for science subchapter C. High school.* Accessed at http://ritter.tea.state.tx.us/rules/tac/chapter112/ch112c .html#112.33 on January 6, 2021.

Thomas, L. (2019, April 26). *7 smart, fast ways to do formative assessment* [Blog post]. Accessed at https:// edutopia.org/article/7-smart-fast-ways-do-formative-assessment on July 14, 2020.

Tomlinson, C. A. (2012). One to grow on / What Heather taught me. *Educational Leadership, 70*(1), 88–89.

Torres, C. (2019). *Assessment as an act of love.* Accessed at www.ascd.org/publications/newsletters/ education-update/feb19/vol61/num02/Assessment-as-an-Act-of-Love.aspx on March 3, 2021.

Tough, P. (2016). *Helping children succeed: What works and why*. Boston: Houghton Mifflin Harcourt.

United Nations Educational, Scientific and Cultural Organization. (n.d.). *Global citizenship education*. Accessed at https://en.unesco.org/themes/gced on January 6, 2021.

Wagner, T. (2014). *The global achievement gap: Why our kids don't have the skills they need for college, careers, and citizenship—and what we can do about it* (Rev. ed.). New York: Perseus Books Group.

Wagner, T., & Dintersmith, T. (2015). *Most likely to succeed: Preparing our kids for the innovation era*. New York: Scribner.

Wakabayashi, D. (2019, May 28). *Google's shadow work force: Temps who outnumber full-time employees*. Accessed at www.nytimes.com/2019/05/28/technology/google-temp-workers.html on July 29, 2020.

Walker, T. (2014). *The testing obsession and the disappearing curriculum*. Accessed at http://neatoday.org /2014/09/02/the-testing-obsession-and-the-disappearing-curriculum-2 on August 12, 2020.

Warner, J. (2017, August 10). *Self-assessment leads to rigor/self-regulation* [Blog post]. Accessed at www .insidehighered.com/blogs/just-visiting/self-assessment-leads-rigorself-regulation on September 9, 2020.

Wasserman, S. (2009). *Teaching for thinking today: Theory, strategies, and activities for the K–8 classroom*. New York: Teachers College Press.

WeAreTeachers Staff. (2016, April 27). *11 research project strategies for second graders: Real teachers share their best ideas!* [Blog post]. Accessed at https://weareteachers.com/best-of-teacher-helpline-11 -research-project-strategies-for-second-graders on July 14, 2020.

Webber, M. A. (2019). *Looking up! What is our place in the universe? An astronomy UbD for 8th grade*. Accessed at https://digitalcommons.trinity.edu/educ_understandings/445 on January 5, 2021.

West Windsor-Plainsboro Middle School. (2016). *West Windsor-Plainsboro Middle School global challenge* [Video file]. Accessed at www.youtube.com/watch?v=m7N65U0Ynz8 on January 5, 2021.

Wexler, N. (2019a). Elementary education has gone terribly wrong. *The Atlantic*. Accessed at www. theatlantic.com /magazine/archive/2019/08/the-radical-case-for-teaching-kids-stuff/592765 on July 14, 2020.

Wexler, N. (2019b). *The knowledge gap: The hidden cause of America's broken education system—and how to fix it*. New York: Avery.

Wiggins, G. (2007, November 15). *What is an essential question?* [Blog post]. Accessed at https:// authenticeducation.org/ae_bigideas/article.lasso?artid=53 on July 14, 2020.

Wiggins, G. (2012). *Seven keys to effective feedback*. Accessed at www.ascd.org/publications/educational -leadership/sept12/vol70/num01/Seven-Keys-to-Effective-Feedback.aspx on January 5, 2021.

Wiggins, G., & McTighe, J. (n.d.). *UbD template 2.0*. Accessed at https://tinyurl.com/y5wo38mz on January 5, 2021.

Wiggins, G., & McTighe, J. (2005). *Understanding by Design* (expanded 2nd ed.). Alexandria, VA: Association for Supervision and Curriculum Development.

Wiggins, G., & McTighe, J. (2011). *The Understanding by Design guide to creating high-quality units.* Alexandria, VA: Association for Supervision and Curriculum Development.

Williams, P. (2017). Student agency for powerful learning. *Knowledge Quest, 45*(4), 8–15.

Willingham, D. T. (2019). *How to teach critical thinking.* Accessed at www.danielwillingham.com /uploads/5/0/0/7/5007325/willingham_2019_nsw_critical_thinking.pdf on August 24, 2020.

Wilson, L. O. (2014). *What are essential questions?* [Blog post]. Accessed at https://thesecondprinciple .com/essential-teaching-skills/essential-questions on August 24, 2020.

Winter, J. (2015). *Lillian's right to vote.* New York: Penguin Random House.

Winthrop, R. (2020). *The need for civic education in 21st-century schools.* Accessed at www.brookings.edu /policy2020/bigideas/the-need-for-civic-education-in-21st-century-schools on January 6, 2021.

Wolpert-Gawron, H. (2017). *Getting critical about critical thinking.* Accessed at www.edutopia.org/blog/ getting-critical-about-critical-thinking-heather-wolpert-gawron on March 1, 2021.

World Health Organization. (2020, April 17). *Q&A on coronaviruses (COVID-19).* Accessed at www.who .int/emergencies/diseases/novel-coronavirus-2019/question-and-answers-hub/q-a-detail/q-a -coronaviruses on August 22, 2020.

Wormeli, R. (2005). *Summarization in any subject: 50 techniques to improve student learning.* Alexandria, VA: Association for Supervision and Curriculum Development.

Zook, C. (2018, November 1). *What is a curriculum map . . . and how do you make one?* [Blog post]. Accessed at www.aeseducation.com/blog/what-is-a-curriculum-map-and-how-do-you-make-one on January 2, 2021.

Index

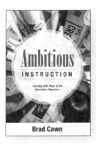

Ambitious Instruction
Brad Cawn

Discover a blueprint for making rigor visible, accessible, and actionable in grades 6–12 classrooms. *Ambitious Instruction* guides readers toward using the twin tenets of problem-based learning and synthesis to significantly strengthen students' ability to read, write, and think within and across disciplines.
BKF842

Raising the Rigor
Eileen Depka

This user-friendly resource shares questioning strategies and techniques proven to enhance students' critical-thinking skills, deepen their engagement, and better prepare them for college and careers. The author also provides a range of templates, surveys, and checklists for planning instruction, deconstructing academic standards, and increasing classroom rigor.
BKF722

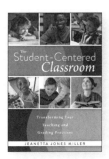

The Student-Centered Classroom
Jeanetta Jones Miller

Student-centered classrooms allow schools to fulfill their most enduring promise: to give students a fair chance to grow up literate, open-minded, and prepared to succeed. Begin making this critically important shift in your classroom with this resource as your guide.
BKF951

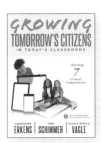

Growing Tomorrow's Citizens in Today's Classrooms
Cassandra Erkens, Tom Schimmer, and Nicole Dimich

For students to succeed in an ever-changing world, they must acquire unique knowledge and skills. Practical and research based, this resource will help educators design assessment and instruction to ensure students master critical competencies, including collaboration, critical thinking, creative thinking, communication, digital citizenship, and more.
BKF765

Solution Tree | Press
a division of
Solution Tree

Visit SolutionTree.com or call 800.733.6786 to order.

Wait! Your professional development journey doesn't have to end with the last pages of this book.

We realize improving student learning doesn't happen overnight. And your school or district shouldn't be left to puzzle out all the details of this process alone.

No matter where you are on the journey, we're committed to helping you get to the next stage.

Take advantage of everything from **custom workshops** to **keynote presentations** and **interactive web and video conferencing**. We can even help you develop an action plan tailored to fit your specific needs.

Let's get the conversation started.

Call 888.763.9045 today.

SolutionTree.com